me! me! me!:

How #Millennials Will Save the American Workplace

by

Danielle Shepherd, Ph.D.

Published by Nicroix Publishing, LLC
Cleveland, Ohio 44106

me! me! me!: How Millennials Will Save the American
Workplace
ISBN - 978-0-578-43347-9

me! me! me!

Table of Contents

Contents

Authors Note

The information within this book should not be used as a means to diagnose one's self as being afflicted with Narcissistic Personality Disorder (NPD). This book provides a general and broad description of characteristics, attributes, and behaviors associated with narcissism, as a broader context within the scope of a new leadership form. Simply put, this book is meant to introduce and expand our understanding of Transformative Narcissism not to diagnose NPD. The measurement of Transformative Narcissism is possible through a lengthy assessment which should be administered and scored by a trained professional. The information provided in this book is based on academic research conducted by the author but should be used as informative and not treated as a textbook. For more academically appropriate information on the topics within this book, refer to the author's dissertation, which can be found in the Notes section.

me! me! me!

Introduction

In today's social climate it is not out of the ordinary to hear someone referred to as "being" narcissistic. To some degree, it appears as though some people strive to be referred to as such. Therefore, I found it imperative to introduce a version of narcissism that has remained hidden in the shadows and deemed the negative personality type of anyone displaying self-absorbed behavior or a "Me Me Me" personality. In the next nine chapters of this book, you will be introduced to a healthy perspective on narcissism in combination with Transformational Leadership and how it has evolved within the Millennial (aka Gen Y) generation – which I have named Transformative Narcissism.

You will see it stated multiple times throughout the book that the information provided is not meant to diagnose Narcissistic Personality Disorder (NPD) and is not based on the condition of NPD. Transformative Narcissism is based on "healthy" levels of narcissism as a personality trait, which basically means that there is a number on a scale that an individual must fall between to qualify as someone who could **possibly** be a Transformative Narcissist. There is a specific score of transformational leadership and a necessary score on the productive narcissism assessment that is needed to determine if someone is a Transformative Narcissist. In short, there is a very detailed process to statistically determine if someone theoretically could be or is a Transformative Narcissist.

If you have picked up this book, then some part of you is curious about Millennials, and what role they will play in saving the American workplace. Many people who read this book will be surprised that the "master plan" involves narcissism. This book is the first introduction to the idea of Transformative Narcissism, and some readers may find themselves unfamiliar with the multiple styles of leadership mentioned in this book, so I've provided you with some assistance. At the end of the Introduction and before Chapter One there is a 'Key Terms' section that will give you the necessary information to move confidently through the book. And for those who are interested in academically related references to the topics mentioned throughout the book, there is a 'Notes' section at the back of the book just for you!

My intention among others when deciding to write this book was to take an overly complex topic and make it simple. I wanted the introduction to Transformative Narcissism to be easily understood. I wanted to remove all of the necessary but overly academic information from my dissertation and put it in a reader-friendly book. I think that was achieved (or that could be my narcissism talking). This book is meant to be less business slacks double-expresso, and more yoga pants avocado toast style. The purpose of this book is to break away from the negative stereotypes associated with narcissism and Millennials. Narcissism can be healthy, and Millennials are more than self-entitled, know it all's. Millennials are the star of the show, but this book also pays homage to the two other primary generations within the workforce. Millennials are here to save the day, but it is a team effort. Baby Boomers and Gen Xer's are necessary components in this proposed plan to change the American workplace and maybe even the world. I even made sure to include the history of the American workplace as it pertains to the Silent generation and the future of the workplace with Gen Z – to provide a more clear overall picture of the future workplace.

me! me! me!

I am sure that my relaxed introduction may cause some people a little concern on my qualifications to write this book — I am a 30s something Millennial after all, what could I possibly know, right? Don't worry I am a highly trained professional! I spent 3 of 4 years on my research while working on my Ph.D. in Organizational Leadership at the Chicago School of Professional Psychology. I passed my comprehensive exams on the first try, passed my dissertation defense with No Changes (that's a really big deal, so I am told), and finished with a 4.0 G.PA. I am considered an expert in Productive Narcissism and Millennial Leadership. Add to all of that a Masters in Law, a Certification in Cross-Cultural Management, a Certification in Intelligence, and a B.A. in My Parents Made Me go to College. I have been a small business owner for over nine years in construction. I promise that it isn't as glamorous as it seems. Over that period of time, I have managed to own multiple businesses, ranging from the restaurant industry to the nonprofit sector.

I have experienced success, and I have experienced failure, but through it all, I have managed not to be distracted by the good and to persevere through the bad. Who better to explain Millennial Leadership than an overly educated Millennial leader? Some of the principles in this book may make you uncomfortable and seem outlandish, but every great idea that changed the world was initially met with those same exact feelings and thoughts.

This book may not change the world, but if it just starts the conversation and inspires people to destroy the box that we seem destined to remain in, then this book will have done what it was intended to do. Now please, go change into your comfy pants and get ready for a page-turner, because you thought you knew

me! me! me!

Millennials but you had no idea of just what they can do to transform the world!

Key Terms

∞ The 5 Generational Groups
- ⊕ Silent Generation born 1900-1945
- ⊕ Baby Boomers born 1946-1964
- ⊕ Generation X born 1965-1980
- ⊕ Millennials also known as Generation Y born 1981-2000
- ⊕ Generation Z also referred to as Nexters born after 2000.

∞ Productive Narcissism – A leadership style practiced by an individual with a narcissistic dominant personality, and driven by a vision to promote significant change.

∞ Transformational Leadership – A style of leadership where the leader identifies necessary change and creates a vision to generate this change through inspiration and from the commitment of others.

me! me! me!

∞ Transformative Narcissist (Trans narcissist) – A leader who embodies both productive narcissism and transformational leadership. A leader with a narcissistic dominant personality who inspires and drives commitment from others to achieve their vision for significant change.

∞ Transformative Narcissism (Trans Narcissism) – A leadership style utilizes the strengths and balances the limitations of productive narcissism with the follower oriented focus of transformational leadership to drive a vision for significant change.

Danielle Shepherd

Chapter One:

Millennials are BAE

In 2016, Microsoft sent out an email to some of their interns. The title read, "Hey BAE Intern! <3" and it advertised a "chill party" with "hella noms," "lots of dranks," and beer pong with the tagline: "Hell yes to getting lit on a Monday night." It was not well-received. Other companies and businesses have attempted to entice Millennial customers in similar ways. For example, a 2017 Pepsi commercial failed in its attempt to connect with Millennials by connecting Kendall Jenner and the Black Lives Matter movement – with a very negative response. This all goes to show that Millennials are one of the most misunderstood generations. No one seems to know quite how to grow and support them, much less appreciate the way that they think.

Danielle Shepherd

Millennials are often described as too tied to their smartphones, very easily offended and fragile, responding to criticism in an overly-negative way, complaining about their lives – though older generations seem to think they've had it easier, acting as if their perspective and experiences are the only ones that are valid, wanting credit for 'trying hard' instead of actually accomplishing something, and arrogant about their own ignorance. Add to this that Millennials are perceived to be 'entitled' – to think that the world 'owes' them something and that they are generally over-educated. The list goes on. All of this makes it difficult for Millennials to begin in an entry position in the workplace – they have to deal with others' preconceived notions about who they are.

Most of all, Millennials are perceived to be 'entitled' – to think that everything will be handed to them or come easily. They seem to have unrealistic expectations about the world and believe that all they have to do is "try hard" and they will be rewarded.

But, do all Millennials share these traits? And if they do, are these characteristics necessarily a bad thing – or are they simply different from the characteristics of previous generations. The context in which this seems to matter most is the workplace.

Although you may not have noticed exactly *how*, the American workplace has changed. For the first time in history, there are three generational groups working together – Baby Boomers, Gen-Xers, and Millennials – instead of two. In other words, in most workplaces across the country, there are three completely different world-views competing with one another in the same environment. Baby Boomers generally remain focused on their work as an important part of life. They are goal-oriented, worry about fairness and equality of opportunity. They are also competitive and concerned with self-actualization. Gen-Xers, on the other hand, are more individualistic; they grew up along with important technological advancements, which make them technologically proficient. And they are flexible, valuing a balance between life and work that their predecessors thought of differently. In fact, Gen-Xers are highly important in the context of the workplace as they are often in middle management positions – the people who have direct contact with and supervise Millennials.

Millennials, however, the largest group entering the workforce, seem to be a mystery to their generational counterparts. Ask a Baby Boomer or a Gen-Xer about Millennials and they'll likely begin to complain. This is because Millennials are often perceived negatively by previous generations.

So, the important question arises: How can we better understand Millennials in a business context? How are Millennials motivated when it comes to the working world? What are their leadership styles? How should Millennials be handled, supported, and trained? How can we help Millennials to grow in the current workplace environment?

As a Millennial, I've thought about these problems quite a bit. No one seems to have the answer. When I hear people complaining about Millennial colleagues, I wonder whether the problem lies in a lack of understanding about how Millennials work and how they think about the world in general. If corporations have a hard time simply advertising to Millennials effectively, then how can workplace communication effectively occur across generations? There seems to be a serious disconnect.

For me, the answer to many of these questions lies in comprehending one key component of Millennial psychology: narcissism. Through my research as an Industrial-organizational psychologist, I have discovered that a particular kind of narcissism (*transformative narcissism*) is a characteristic that many Millennials share – and, believe it or not, it is a *healthy* kind of narcissism. When applied to leadership techniques, leaders who are transformative narcissists (which is also referred to as trans narcissism) can pave the way for significant change and transform their workplace in positive ways. Transformative narcissists possess the ability to get others to follow their vision – and they believe that their vision is strong enough to change the world. They have the social intelligence to influence others and can thus accomplish great things. Unlike ordinary narcissists, transformative narcissists are grounded in reality; they are risk takers, unique leaders, and strong individuals.

This book investigates the possibility that transformative narcissism, as a trait of Millennials, can help to identify effective leaders in the workplace. I have written this book with three hopes in mind: 1) that Millennials will read it and understand how to become more successful business leaders, 2) that Baby Boomers and Gen-Xers will use it as a guide to comprehending how Millennials think and operate in the working world, and 3) that this book will help to confront and break the negative stereotype associated with the word 'narcissism' and help us to expand our understanding of it beyond its negative connotation.

Think about it. What if the most commonly cited negative trait of the Millennial generation could be perceived as *positive* as opposed to *negative*? What if, in other words, Millennials had just the right combination of specific traits to take both the good and bad aspects of narcissism and turn them into productivity - and ultimately GREAT leadership?

Imagine the very landscape of the American workplace transformed. Millennials have the capacity -

and the talent – to do this in a *positive* way. This very thing could happen if Millennials were given the support, resources, and opportunity for growth that they need. Just think of it. Good leaders often share a specific and unique trait: they have a vision and they want to involve everyone in making that vision happen. Transformative narcissism, as you will see in the following chapters, is different from the kind of narcissism that we normally think of negatively. Unlike an ordinary narcissist, a person who is concerned with what pertains to them, a transformative narcissist is grounded in reality. What does this mean? It means that *transformative narcissists* can influence other people, create great change, and make things happen! They are able to rally others around their specific vision – and bring it to fruition. This means that a *transformative narcissist* can, like no other kind of person, accomplish great things in the workplace.

me! me! me!

Studies, like mine, concerning Millennials show that Millennials have an increase in this kind of narcissistic behaviors – the productive and transformational kind! Allowing Millennials to tap into their transformative narcissistic tendencies could result in a new kind of leadership – not one that is virtuous, follower-oriented, ideal, or grounded in emotional intelligence, but relies instead on vision, risk-taking, and divergent thinking. Transformative narcissists like productive narcissists, have a disregard for societal boundaries and social conformity – and thus have the unique power to transform our way of thinking about the way we do business.

It is imperative to note that the very make-up of transformative narcissism is built upon both productive narcissism and transformational leadership. To appreciate the idea and foundation of transformative leadership one must understand the building blocks of productive narcissism and transformational leadership. The very essence of transformative narcissism is to utilize the strengths and to balance the limitations of productive narcissism with the follower oriented focus of transformational leadership to drive a vision for significant change.

Psychologists and psycho analysts may have identified the concept of a *productive narcissist* rather recently, but these persons have existed – and influenced others – for quite some time. Influential leaders like Napoléon Bonaparte, Mahatma Ghandi, and Franklin Delano Roosevelt were all individuals who influenced others with their visionary ideals. At the beginning of the last century, men like John D. Rockefeller, Henry Ford, Andrew Carnegie, and Thomas Edison were busy changing the face of various American industries – through convincing others to follow their vision for the future. Think of all the productive narcissists that you may know who have become successful because of this very ability to transform the world around them, to stick to their vision and bring others along for an amazing ride.

More recently, entrepreneurs and creative thinkers such as Steve Jobs, Bill Gates, and Andy Groves have shown that being gifted and creative in business amounts to a good strategy. They were able to "see the big picture," to take huge and important risks, to accept the challenge of changing the world according to their own vision. How were they able to do this? These figures all had one thing in common – they share traits of a productive narcissist.

If we want American business to continue to be competitive in the current workplace climate, then we need visionaries to lead us. We need people with big ideas, people willing to take huge risks, people who are willing to think creatively about solving new problems.

Danielle Shepherd

We need Millennials. We need *transformative narcissists*. Transformative narcissists will change the world because they aren't afraid to take the kind of risks that can make a huge impact on others around them. They are unafraid – because of their transformative narcissism. Millennials who are transformative narcissists have a strange and wonderful power; they often think that they can't lose, that they need to take such large risks for the simple fact that no one else will. Baby Boomers and Gen-Xers have a great work ethic and many other positive qualities. Some of them have already changed the world with their own, unique vision of the future. Yet, there are more individuals who think this way that are Millennials. All of the things that you think of as negative when it comes to Millennials when viewed in the right context are really positive – their way of doing things results in an increase in productivity and in grand, world-changing vision for what's next. We just need to learn to harness those amazing abilities.

So, whether you're a Baby Boomer CEO, a Gen-X manager, or a Millennial just starting out in the workforce, it will be helpful to you to understand where Millennials are coming from – and that the traits you think of as negative are really *positive*! Bringing together the three generations that are currently working in businesses across the country is important. We all need to understand one another, especially how to create an environment of understanding through ingenuity, communication, and knowledge. Then, the next time that you hear someone speaking negatively about how Millennials are self-centered narcissists, you can reply, "Yes, of course they are! But, some of them are *transformative narcissists* and that's a good thing! They make really excellent leaders!" This is why Millennials are BAE – because, by "Brilliantly Advancing Everyone," they hold the key to the future of new businesses and leadership models that are led by vision, explode with creativity, drive ingenuity, and reintroduce work satisfaction and happiness back to the workplace.

me! me! me!

Chapter Two

Reflection Perfection:

Into Narcissus' Pond

The word 'narcissism' comes from an ancient Greek tale. According to legend, Narcissus, the son of the river god and his beloved nymph, thought so highly of himself that he did not care for those who loved him. The god Nemesis decided to teach Narcissus a lesson and led him to a pond in which Narcissus could see his own reflection. Immediately, Narcissus fell in love with his own image – so much so that he never wanted to leave the pond, leave his own reflection, and died there because of his obsession with himself.

When you think of a narcissist, you probably don't think of the Greek legend. Instead, you think of that person you know who is completely in love with themselves. Maybe they have difficulty passing up a mirror without taking a look; maybe they constantly talk about how good-looking or smart they are – and how everyone else is so beneath them. Narcissists are all around us. In fact, I'm sure you know more than one. Everything in their life has to do with what is going on with them. It's never about anyone else or anyone else's needs. Narcissists, true narcissists, cannot see past their own noses. They crave the attention of others – and, strangely, their validation. You can spot a narcissist quite easily: just look for the person who thinks that they are better than everyone else, they push the idea that they are the smartest person in the room, and even though you may find them obnoxious they have the ability to draw you in.

Think of the last time you went to a party or gathering. Was there one person there, maybe more than one, who simply couldn't get enough of the spotlight? Who made sure that they got everyone's attention? Who seemed to scream "Look at me!"? Who oozed confidence like it was perspiration? That person could have been someone with a number of "attention seeking" traits of which one was narcissism.

Or, when we think of someone like Steve Jobs, who was able to strike the right balance between the negative aspects of narcissism and the positive, or productive, aspects and we begin to understand how narcissism could be a positive thing. In fact, many Millennials have narcissistic traits, but lack the ability to balance them with other aspects of their working life in order to be productive – in other words, they lack the ability to channel their narcissism for good. Transformative narcissism, as we will see, is about balancing the good parts of narcissism with its limitations. Transformative narcissists are still narcissists. They struggle to contain their narcissistic side, not allowing it to dominate their productive and transformational leadership style. When people talk about the sometimes brutal management practices of Steve Jobs, they are right to think that narcissism had a part to play in that severe style. However, we must also admit that what came from those practices changed the world – one device at a time. Steve Jobs was a productive narcissist because he was a narcissist who was able to maintain a balance between the good and bad parts of his narcissistic personality. As with everything over time, narcissism has evolved. Productive narcissists, such as Jobs, have set the stage for Millennials to move past productive narcissism into transformative narcissism!

It should be clear, though, that everyone who you might call a 'narcissist' could be diagnosed as having narcissistic personality disorder from a clinical perspective. In 1898, Havelock Ellis coined the term 'narcissism' by describing it as a clinical condition of "perverse self-love." Sigmund Freud took this idea further, describing narcissism as a personality type with certain characteristics like unflappable strength, confidence, and sometimes arrogance. Many other psychologists and students of psychology have tried to refine the definition of narcissism in order to more easily identify narcissists in society. Sometimes, narcissists have been described as "outgoing;" they have also been located in top management and leadership positions because they have the need to acquire prestige, power, and glamour. In addition, hiring committees (and other individuals and groups) are actually more likely to gravitate toward candidates who display narcissistic traits – especially when handling new hires and promotions. Narcissists are preoccupied with themselves. If we look to the Diagnostic and

Statistical Manual of Mental Disorders, we find that narcissism can involve "grandiosity, a need for admiration and attention from others, exaggerated self-importance, a preoccupation with fantasies of unlimited success, power or brilliance, envy, entitlement, exploitativeness, limited empathy, and arrogance."

Take, for example, one version of an old fable that is often used to show how narcissists lack the ability to care about others. They are often manipulative and will be nice to anyone – as long as they are useful to them. I'm talking, of course, about the old story of the "Scorpion and the Frog." In this story, a frog and a scorpion happen to be standing on the same riverbank. The frog is able to swim and can navigate the river very easily. However, the scorpion will need help to cross the river because it cannot swim and could easily drown in its attempt. So, the scorpion decides to ask the frog to let him ride on his back across the river. The frog considers this proposition and asks the scorpion, "But if I give you a ride across the river, how do I know that you won't sting me? Scorpions are known to sting and if you sting me, I will surely die." The scorpion assures the frog that he will not sting him if he gets him safely across the river, so the frog agrees. Now, just as they reach the banks of the river and the scorpion knows he will be safe, he stings the frog. The frog protests and says, "You promised that you wouldn't sting me if I helped you to get to the other side safely!" Smiling with pleasure, the scorpion replies, "You knew what I was when you let me ride on your back."

In this example, the scorpion (a narcissist) uses the frog to get what he needs, manipulates the poor frog into helping him, and then goes against his word and kills the frog with his venomous sting in the end. This is how narcissists are traditionally viewed. Just like the scorpion, you can't trust a narcissist to keep their word unless it involves a benefit to them. Even if you trust narcissists, they rarely care whether or not they hurt you – it's all about them! Then, inevitably, narcissists end up damaging the person who allowed them into their lives. The narcissist is just like the scorpion – harmful and dangerous. When individuals do not care about anything but themselves, when they believe that they have the right to manipulate others just to get what they want, then they are truly narcissistic, in love with their own reflection and lacking any empathy for others.

This is the *clinical* definition of narcissism. It's the one that psychologists and other mental health professionals use to diagnose their patients with a certain kind of problem with their personality. This is also what most people think of when they think of a 'narcissist.' They might think that narcissists are difficult to deal with because they don't really care about anyone but themselves. Maybe they think that narcissists are just arrogant jerks not worth having to deal with, especially in an office setting. However, there is another kind of narcissism – 'healthy' or 'transformative' narcissism.

Because there are so many different ways to describe how a narcissist behaves, it is difficult to find a definition of narcissism that is not negative or does not have negative connotations. People across the globe have been diagnoses with narcissism – it's a pretty well-distributed problem around the world. This suggests that narcissistic people exist in every society and in every country on the Earth. However, as bad as the negative definition of narcissism can be – and as difficult as it is to deal with a narcissist's behavior, which can cause extreme discomfort to those exposed to the narcissist, there can be a healthy form of narcissism. To be clear, however, though narcissism is distributed across cultures, continents, and age groups, less than 1%

of the worldwide population has been diagnosed with this extreme, or true, version of narcissism – narcissistic personality disorder. It is much more common for individuals who display some narcissistic traits to be called "narcissists," even though they could never be true narcissists in the sense of having narcissistic personality disorder.

Sometimes, people who are arrogant or self-involved (like narcissists are) are called narcissists in this clinical way. It is more difficult than we may imagine being a full-fledged narcissist. For people who truly have narcissistic personality disorder, narcissism is usually a gateway to more serious psychological disorders such as psychopathy and sociopathy. In those cases, narcissism would be the best, "warmest and fuzziest" part of their cluster of personality issues. Some scholars have called the alternative version of narcissism "mature narcissism" and have said that it can bring about behaviors that are enjoyable, like vision and creativity. "Mature narcissism" is, as we can see, quite different from the diagnosis of narcissistic personality disorder. Some have even said that narcissism can be a healthy and essential process in normal psychological development.

These positive behaviors, 'healthy' or 'adaptive' narcissism, have even been said to be beneficial to those individuals who hold positions of leadership and/or authority. Who wouldn't want a leader who is confident in his or her own abilities? In fact, most people do not want leaders who are meek and lack confidence. This is where healthy narcissism can come into play in a positive way.

It may sound strange to talk about narcissism as 'good.' Most of us do not like to deal with narcissists in our daily lives - they seem to create drama and are difficult to work with, especially in a business setting.

Millennials are the generation most accused of narcissism. Jean Twenge has even said that there is a "narcissism epidemic" among Millennials. Millennials, people say, are self-absorbed, overly self-confident, and often referred to as the "look at me" generation. So, how can we view narcissism as a good thing? Isn't it usually considered a kind of personality disorder? Why would anyone want to encourage these characteristics in another person much less work with someone who possesses these attributes?

The simple fact is that *healthy narcissism* is different from the kind of narcissism that most people deal with as a mental health issue. Productive narcissists are people who have the kind of personality type that allow them to deal with crises, to lead in a time of rapid social and economic change. Productive narcissists have strengths that others do not possess – things like perseverance, awareness of threats, charisma, a sense of humor, and a voracious appetite for learning. However, even a productive narcissist can be extremely sensitive to criticism, paranoid at times, prone to anger, have a limited capacity for listening to others, and have an extreme sense of competitiveness. All of these characteristics, when taken together, are the kind of personality traits that make for good leaders.

It's important to know about narcissism – and its potential positive effects in the workplace – because the last twenty-five years of research have shown that there has been a distinct increase in narcissistic behaviors in younger generations. Whereas Baby Boomers are often accused of having an impossible work ethic and Gen-Xers had to deal with the stigma of being called apathetic, Millennials are thought to be narcissists. This is true. If narcissism is a commonly shared trait among Millennials, then the trick of studying this generation as it pertains to leadership and the workplace is to develop ways to grow the positive aspects of Millennials' narcissistic tendencies.

Let me put it another way. To some degree, the purpose of studying leadership is to figure out what works and what is no longer working when it comes to leadership roles. We need to emulate what works and get rid of what doesn't. Right now, many of the Millennials who are entering the workforce, the new generation that is beginning to stream into businesses and offices around the globe, have narcissistic characteristics and some are narcissists. In order to understand how we can progress as far as leadership is concerned, we need to figure out who will be leading – and what kind of leaders they will be.

What I really want to propose is that there is another kind of leadership that is possible – one that is not virtuous, follower-oriented, ideal, or governed by what we call 'emotional intelligence,' but one that relies heavily on vision, taking risks, divergent thinking, and the disregard for societal boundaries and social conformity. Let's think about this for a moment. What would the American workplace look like if an entire, new generation of people, a generation that sees the world differently, were to take their place in leadership? The current way that businesses are run is primarily hierarchical – top down. No one really thinks about stepping 'outside of the box' or thinking of new and inventive ways to lead a particular company. Millennials who are transformative narcissists, are capable of seeing beyond that vision. They have seen what their parents and grandparents did, witnessed what they accomplished, and want something more. Millennials, because they are often transformative narcissists, do not feel bound by the same societal and social boundaries that members of other generations do. Truly, they have vision.

Let's look at an example of this kind of transformative narcissism. For instance, when we look at the way that the aftermath of natural disasters are handled, we can see that the kind of leadership needed is very important. A bureaucratic and hierarchical corporate culture that lacks true leadership that someone like a transformative narcissist could provide, things tend to go awry. On the other hand, when transformative narcissists are allowed to flourish, wonderful things can happen – lives may even be saved. When Hurricane Katrina hit the city of New Orleans in 2005, the Federal Emergency Management Agency (FEMA) was a hierarchical, bureaucratic governmental agency. The leadership in place was "top down." This meant that, for anything to get done within the agency, each person (from the bottom up) had to get permission from their superior. At one point, many families who lost their homes due to flooding had to wait for weeks for emergency trailers to be delivered - because new employees had not completed their sexual harassment training. In fact, the then director of FEMA, Michael Brown, did not even know that there were people trapped in the Superdome until a news reporter asked him about it during an interview. In this situation, the person at the top had no idea what was actually happening on the ground - a bad thing for a governmental agency tasked with saving and preserving lives!

On the other hand, the U.S. Coast Guard had the same kind of responsibilities toward the people in New Orleans and the surrounding areas: to help save lives and rescue those in need. But, the Coast Guard had a different kind of organizational setup. Their motto is "rescue first, ask permission later." So, each member of the USCG was able to make decisions - on their own - about how they would deal with situations as they presented themselves. They had the freedom to use the knowledge they had of what was happening *right then* to make decisions. No one in the USCG had to ask permission before they rescued someone from the top of a roof; no one had to ask permission before they were allowed to save someone from the rising waters. The USCG was simply allowed to do their job – help people. In fact, after what happened during Katrina, the U.S. government realized that there were problems with the way that FEMA was run – and hired a former U.S. Coast Guard Admiral to make things better. The government came to this conclusion, citing that the way the USCG did things was *better*, it was more effective. The organizational style of the USCG was more efficient and did not cling to the 'old' ways of hierarchical business models. Thus, things improved for FEMA.

Millennials who are transformative narcissists could be compared to the people working in the USCG.

me! me! me!

Transformational leadership does just that – *transforms.* If everyone clings to the same, old, way of doing things, then nothing will ever change. And productive narcissists are the very people who have been effective in bringing about great, and at times necessary, change. Productive narcissism is highly connected to transformational leadership in positive ways thus creating the very idea of transformative narcissism. We have to look at these foundational principles of transformative narcissism and discover how to build a solid argument for this leadership form. Let's take a closer look at how narcissism can be healthy.

Danielle Shepherd

Chapter Three

True Vision:

Narcissism Can Be Healthy

We now know that narcissism has long been considered unhealthy. People, who are narcissists, in the traditional sense of the word, are not desirable people to be around. They only consider themselves and have trouble making room for anyone else in their lives. If we look at how this particular personality trait translates into the workplace, it seems unlikely that anyone would want to hire a narcissist, much less work with them on a daily basis. This is completely understandable; employees and employers who are narcissists are difficult to get along with. They simply don't have the kind of 'fit' that is acceptable in the workplace.

Narcissists exploit the people around them, have an overblown sense of themselves, and need constant validation from those within their environment.

However, as I have already discussed, there exists a 'healthy' version of narcissism – a trait that could be seen as desirable in a leader. There are many different ways to view narcissism – both negative and positive. Here, I want to explore more positive ways to view narcissistic traits, understanding that they can lead to transformational and visionary changes in leadership roles in the workplace. Sometimes, 'healthy' narcissism is called 'mature narcissism' because this kind of narcissism can bring about behaviors that others want to see in the person who leads them. A mature, or healthy, narcissist can bring levels of creativity and vision to the workplace, making them very effective leaders. In fact, healthy narcissism can be seen, not as a negative, but as beneficial to anyone who holds a position of leadership and authority.

It is true that there are few researchers who accept that there is a 'healthy' kind of narcissism. But, scholars, like me, who choose to look beyond narcissism as a personality disorder, have come to realize that there are people in the world who are technically narcissists, but offer something more. The simple truth is that narcissistic characteristics, when in a healthy form, can cause a person to exhibit ambition, creativity, and growth. This means that a healthy narcissist can bring these same things to the workplace in the form of effective leadership.

Let's explore, however, the different and competing perspectives on narcissism so that we can better understand what healthy narcissism really is – and how it relates to Millennials in the workplace. A scholar named Jean Twenge, for example, has explored and researched the millennial generation and their connection with what Twenge calls the current "narcissism epidemic." Many members of other generations have made it a point to complain about the supposed 'narcissism' of Millennials. People will say that Millennials are all about themselves, entitled, were given too many participation trophies growing up, do not know the value of hard work, and try to 'skate by' while putting in the minimum amount of effort. What Twenge, and others, have argued is that a healthy form of narcissism cannot exist. The popular perspective on narcissism is that it is an antisocial behavior, and this is certainly not a positive thing in the workplace or a positive quality for a leader to have. If that were actually true, then we would have to agree with those researchers and scholars who believe that narcissism is only a personality disorder, that cannot translate into anything good or creative that can only be seen as something undesirable.

But those like Twenge fail to take into consideration that there *are* other kinds of narcissism – and that these can be healthy or mature versions of what was once seen only as an antisocial personality disorder. The way in which I see narcissism, especially when it comes to narcissists in leadership roles, is very different. I see narcissism, not as a personality disorder, but as a characteristic or personality type related to normal personality development and leadership. To clarify: the kind of narcissist that I will explore does not have a personality *disorder*, but scores at the perfect balancing point of the narcissism scale and possesses certain characteristics that make them great leaders, such as transformational leadership. Productive narcissists have vision; they are the people with the best personality type to lead others in a time of rapid social and economic changes. But transformative narcissists go beyond being a visionary because of their transformational <u>and</u> narcissistic characteristics, making it a personality type that can lead, transform, and *inspire* during times of significant change.

Take a look at what is happening in the world today. From large corporations to small businesses, there are new and interesting challenges. Not the least of these is the transformation of the workplace. Some of these changes have been good and some of them have been difficult to navigate. Even the largest, most popular company could suddenly find themselves having to deal with a rapidly changing social, economic, or technological world. How can these businesses survive? The old model of business, the one that most Baby Boomers and Gen Xers have become accustomed to are no longer effective or significantly lack efficiency. Compared to before, it is less common now for an individual to graduate from college, begin working with a particular company or business, and remain there until retirement. Even pensions and retirement programs are becoming a thing of the past. Today's workplace is fast-paced and de-centralized. More people than ever are not working in brick and mortar offices. Instead, they can now work from nearly anywhere – primarily places that provide them with access to the Internet.

This radical change in the way we work occurred because of technological advances. In the early 1990s, the Internet was something that very few people knew about and fewer people knew how to use it. The rise of social media and other platforms has changed not only the way that we see the world and how we are better connected to one another, but also the way that we work. For example, Steve Jobs was the first visionary leader to allow his employees to 'play' while at work. Apple offices included ping pong tables and employees were able to wear whatever attire they liked to work. This was in stark contrast to the way that, say, IBM was at the time. Jobs used to call those who worked at IBM "the suits" because the overtly male, bureaucratic, and hierarchical corporate culture at IBM required them to wear black suits with white shirts and black ties. Jobs wanted to disrupt this kind of corporate culture and image. I'm certain that he received a lot of pushback for coming up with this idea. Now, places like Google and Facebook have taken the idea of a comfortable workplace into account. At Google, for example, employees not only enjoy free food and a casual work environment, but also things like nap pods!

What visionaries like Steve Jobs show us is that thinking outside of the norm when it comes to workplace traditions can actually boost productivity. He knew that the people that worked with him would be happier and more productive if they were allowed to be themselves while at work. He also knew that creating a corporate culture that stifled creativity would be bad for business. The most important element of business is productivity. Productivity equals money and majority of businesses either exist to make money or need money to accomplish their objective. Leaders like Steve Jobs are prime examples of productive narcissists. Why? Because leaders of this kind have charisma, they learn quickly and are hungry for new information, and they persevere. Steve Jobs was a primary force in changing the way that corporate cultures operate. He did this by refusing to listen to anyone else when they gave him advice about how to accomplish his vision. Jobs had a vision and was able to bring it to life by being aware of the world around him and acting accordingly. He was highly aware of threats as well – and therefore able to deal with them in an efficient and productive manner. Jobs implemented a proactive response to threats. It is true that productive narcissism is not an *entirely* positive trait. Productive narcissists, even Steve Jobs, could be considered extremely sensitive to criticism, paranoid, quick to anger, and extremely competitive. However, even these characteristics can possess a positive spin if we look at them from a particular point of view. Each positive and negative trait of the productive narcissist is two sides of the same coin. An individual who is sensitive to criticism will also be able to react more quickly to it and change things for the better; someone who is 'paranoid' might simply be more aware of external threats than others who are not; a person who is extremely competitive will be more willing to push themselves and others to achieve greatness.

Over the last 25 years, researchers have determined that narcissistic personality traits are on the rise. This means that Millennials are more narcissistic than other generations before them, and if things progress in the same manner, this would imply that later generations will become more narcissistic over time. Studies that have been conducted about this upward trend of narcissistic traits in younger generations have focused on trying to prevent narcissism from becoming a problematic issue in society or in the workplace. However, I suggest that preventing narcissism is not the answer – we should, instead, learn how to use narcissistic personality traits to our advantage. We must understand them, and their healthy applications. It is better, I believe, to focus on the positive things that a transformative narcissist can bring to the workplace than trying to change the worldview of younger generations.

The simple fact is that there is another facet to leadership – a new kind of leadership that is not virtuous, follower-oriented, ideal, or governed by emotional intelligence, but a form that relies heavily on vision, taking risks, divergent thinking, and the disregard for societal boundaries and social conformity. In a fast-paced and ever changing world, we need leaders who are critical and creative thinkers. What is a visionary or creative thinker but someone who does not feel bound by the way that things have always been done? Just because things have always been done a certain way, it does not mean that it is the best way. Just think of how many inventors, artists, politicians, and others there are who have changed the world just by seeing it differently.

Transformative narcissists do just that – see the world in a different way. They exist outside of the current normal. This is the key to all kinds of innovation. When innovation truly happens, it can be world changing. Just think of all the ways in which life would be different, and more difficult, if innovation did not exist! To some degree, the very fiber of being an inventor requires traits found in productive and transformative narcissists. While others are dreaming in grey scale, those with visionary traits are dreaming of their vision in full color. They have true vision in the sense of identifying a problem or issue – and then doing something about it.

It is difficult to imagine all the ways in which a person who does not conform to societal norms can positively effect change. Every once in a while, we hear a story about someone who has held on to their own beliefs, despite what everyone around them thinks. Their friends may think they're going too far or flying too close to the sun. Most people think that it is better to just go along with what everyone else is doing. They are afraid to rock the boat or to take action in order to avoid causing trouble. Divergent thinkers, and transformative narcissists, prefer to take the less-travelled road. Others perceive their thoughts and actions as visionary because they go against the status quo. However, some divergent thought and visionary achievements eventually *become* the status quo. Think of Galileo and how his ideas were not readily accepted. If it were not for him we would still believe that all things revolved around the Earth. Think of how the ideas in the Declaration of Independence were strange ideas at the time. When creative and divergent thinkers presents ideas to others, they have the charisma and capability to make those ideas understandable. Being creative or divergent, does not just mean being able to make something new, on the contrary, it means that a visionary or divergent thinker, a transformative narcissist, can enable others to see their vision and to see it through. Transformative narcissists are healthy leaders in the workplace because they do not think the same way that others around them do. They think, and act, differently. But this difference is a *good* thing.

me! me! me!

Change cannot occur if everyone thinks the same way all the time. In fact, that's a recipe for things to stay the same.

People often view transformative narcissists as troublesome because they think of divergent thinking as rebellion. Even scholars and researchers who have studied narcissism claim that narcissistic personalities are "antisocial." However, the transformative narcissist's actions and behavior, their thinking, is not antisocial, but simply different and new. Being rebellious is not always a bad thing, sometimes it is simply thinking of things differently than the norm would suggest. When transformative narcissists 'rebel' against the norm, they are not rebelling against any particular person or rule of society or business, but against ideas that no longer work, or are working against productivity. Transformative narcissists, because they have vision and are divergent thinkers, may seem strange or odd to others. Other people may have difficulty, at first, in understanding where they are coming from because it is such a different perspective than the one that they are accustomed to. They may fear the vision of transformative narcissists and seek to keep them from getting their ideas out into the world.

However, this kind of creativity and divergent thinking ought to be celebrated instead of criticized – especially when it comes to Millennials. Older generations think in terms of the 'right' answers or what adheres to the traditional way of doing things. They may be resistant to change and, therefore, resistant to a healthy narcissists' vision. However, there is value in uniqueness and thinking differently. In addition, people who think differently and have visionary qualities also tend to develop a strong sense of self because they have been repeatedly criticized for going against the grain of the rest of society. This is part of the road to becoming a transformative narcissist – and ultimately a great leader. True leadership requires seeing beyond the present circumstances and requires believing in the impossible. No one can do this except for someone who is willing to stand alone, against all odds.

Still, when it comes to the workplace, a narcissist may not always be a transformative or productive narcissist. Success in business or leadership is not guaranteed just because a person with narcissistic tendencies is involved. The kind of narcissism that creates successful leaders is unique and very specific. Not all transformative or productive narcissists will necessarily bring about significant change and reach their highest potential. They may not even be successful, even if they demonstrate the traits of a transformative narcissist. In other words, a leader who is narcissistic but not productive may not be a successful leader. There is a difference between a productive and an unproductive narcissist. The unproductive narcissist, for example, is not going to be the CEO of a global company, nor will he gain the attention of investors or venture capitalists. The reality is that, to lead a company – or even run a business into the ground – the narcissist in question must be a productive or transformative narcissist. This does not mean that all people who are leaders of companies are narcissists. Yet, there is a strong possibility that some narcissists who run companies are productive or even transformative narcissists. Let me explain further.

Productive narcissists, transformative narcissists, and healthy narcissists, are in plain sight. We cannot help but be aware of their presence. Unproductive narcissists fail to act, fail to produce, and fail to be successful. For any personality type to be productive, it is necessary that it remain grounded in reason. This is one thing that is important about productive and transformative narcissists – while unproductive narcissists are at risk of losing their grasp on reason and reality (especially when they begin to succeed in fulfilling their goals), productive and transformative narcissists knows that remaining reasonable and grounded in reality is the only route to success.

In 1941, Sigmund Freud implied that the main characteristic of narcissists as a group is that they do not conform to social norms. They see the world as a place that needs to change and view themselves as the person to implement that change through their vision. Narcissists are, as I have discussed, different from other personality types specifically because of their unique vision. A productive narcissist, as a matter of fact, will tend to create his or her own sense of meaning. However, this 'meaning' must be appealing enough to draw out their abilities and to attract other people. A productive narcissist who cannot convince others to follow their vision is not really a productive narcissist; he or she is unproductive.

Yet, there are many people who believe that there is something wrong with the world and that they have an idea that will change it for the better. What makes the transformative narcissist any different from an average person with a good idea? The difference between transformative narcissists and others who may dream of changing the world is that they *engage others* (those who work for them, believe in them, and follow them) by helping them to get meaning from their vision.

It is a fact of life that everyone wants to believe in something greater than them, that they want to be a part of something important. For example, many companies that follow the enlightened self-interest model of corporate social responsibility take advantage of the fact that human beings desire to be valued, respected, and part of something larger. Ben & Jerry's ice cream, Tom's

me! me! me!

Shoes – and others – are able to retain good employees because people who work there feel that they are part of something that extends beyond what they can do as individuals. Getting people to believe in this vision is the tricky part. Companies and businesses need leaders who can not only explain their vision, but make other people believe in it. With transformative narcissists, those who follow them believe that they are doing something with a greater purpose, finding a way to make the kind of world-changing impact that they seek.

In order to implement change, a transformative narcissist must get everyone on board with their view of how the world should be changed. This is no easy task! It requires allowing individuals to grow at their own pace while, simultaneously, surrendering themselves to the group effort. In order for transformative narcissists to be successful in accomplishing their vision, their followers must relieve themselves of their own assumptions and accept the belief system or vision provided by their transformative narcissistic leader.

There are many wonderful qualities about transformative narcissists. However, there are some that are not quite so desirable. Even though, for example, transformative narcissists pride themselves on being visionaries, they often lack the ability to have inward vision. Their vision for change is so all-consuming that transformative narcissists have a hard time being self-reflective. They do not allow any anxieties, self-doubt, or any hint of guilt to affect their decision-making. In other words, transformative narcissists lack the ability to know themselves as well as they know their followers.

In order to make their vision a reality, a transformative narcissist must maintain complete and total control over an organization or business. This, in turn, can hinder the transformative narcissist's vision. For example, if followers can no longer contribute to moving the vision of the transformative narcissist forward, then things come to a complete halt. If the transformative narcissist takes complete and total control over an organization, this is exactly what can happen. This need to control can have a direct effect on the transformative narcissist's 'inner circle.' To say it differently, the transformative narcissist, very much like the productive narcissist, will likely surround him or herself with people who are 'yes men,' individuals who are afraid to speak out when the leader is wrong or mistaken.

Transformative narcissists are also competitive by nature. Sometimes they are generally competitive and sometimes they are hyper-competitive. A transformative narcissist believes that by making the workplace a competitive environment, creativity will unfold. In the mind of transformative narcissists, this need to be competitive is rationalized because they believe that competition leads to higher creativity and, thus, productivity. The rationale is that, if people work alone and not in teams, then the competition between them will yield a better result. Now, such focus on competitiveness has been shown to work in industries like law, business, and sports. Such industries also have a high number of individuals with narcissistic characteristics. In sum, transformative narcissists use their follower's commitment to their vision and knowledge of their followers to exert control and accomplish their vision. Transformative narcissists also use this control to encourage what they feel is healthy competition in the workplace.

I have explored many different ways of looking at narcissism, but especially transformative narcissism. The difficulty for narcissists is not reaching a high level of success or progressing up the corporate ladder, but being able to maintain their position at the top.

me! me! me!

Productive, healthy, or transformative, narcissists are new and unfamiliar kinds of leaders. True to its form, and its distaste for social conformity, transformative narcissism is able to break through the imaginary boundaries and limitations that we normally associate with 'good' and 'bad' leadership. Transformative narcissism may not be the ideal type of leadership – in the way that we are accustomed to thinking of it – but it is more realistic than the old notion of a leader that does not possess these characteristics. In fact, most high-ranking executives are found to have narcissistic traits, even today. The view of transformative narcissism is largely based on our ability to move beyond current theories of leadership and toward more realistic goals. With the continual advancement of societies across the globe, the fast-paced growth of technology, and a continual eye to transforming organizations for the better, leadership will change. The people who lead will change. The people who follow those leaders and how leadership is accomplished will also change. Only transformative narcissists have the capacity, and the personality traits, to venture into this different and, to older generations, frightening new world.

Perhaps the best trait of transformative narcissists can be summed up in one word: passion. If we look at the history of this word, it comes from the Greek "*entheos*," which means "enthusiasm." It also directly translated to mean "the good within." The ancient Greeks sought to create a world in which human beings could flourish. They wanted, like transformative narcissists, to go beyond the mundane and to accomplish the extraordinary. Passion, we know, is more than productivity. All productive people, it is true, have a spark of lively energy – this is what, perhaps, makes them so productive! It also leads to fresh and lively work. The most productive among us sees his or her life and work as a *discovery*, one that is continually unfolding, and one that always allows their skills to express themselves in their work. Being active is, however, only one part of productivity. Productive people are also resilient – they do not give up or relent when faced with failure.

Many people are not passionate about their work, however. Just take an unofficial poll of your friends and co-workers and you will find that most people do not like their jobs, much less feel passionate about what they are doing. Leaders who are transformative narcissists can change that; they make everyone around them *feel* the passion of what they are trying to accomplish together. John D. Rockefeller once said that money is a means to an end, but that end is only as good as what it is used for. This means that Rockefeller felt it was his duty to make money and then use that money for the good of his fellow man. This required dedication. When a person becomes unfocused or distracted, he or she can become unproductive. It is the ability of the transformative narcissist to maintain a level of productivity that allows him or her to accomplish demanding and, at times, unthinkable goals. For now, it is the Millennials who are filling the role of transformative narcissist in the workplace. It is high time that some myths about Millennials are addressed – and the so-called "workplace gap" in the generations.

me! me! me!

Chapter Four

The Workplace Generation Gap?

You may have noticed it in your own workplace: there are at least three, and in some places up to five, generations currently working in the United States today. As you can imagine, this inter-mingling of generations at work has been the source of a lot of unrest. Younger employees roll their eyes at a good bit of what their older counterparts do and say – and it is no different for the older generations at work. Millennials don't understand Gen Xers who, in turn, don't understand Baby Boomers. Baby Boomers sometimes have to deal with members of the Silent Generation and find themselves in disagreement. All of the generations listed share in common their disregard for Nexter (Gen Z) employees. Nexters are seen as children, and therefore are not really taken into account in the workplace. Such dismissive attitudes are bound to backfire, seeing that Millennials and Nexters are expected to make up 70% of the workplace by 2020. This is because generational affects are important. They color everything that happens in both life and in the business world. Why? Because each generation has their own way of doing and thinking about things. It's no wonder that there are problems and miscommunications between generations when they all have different worldviews. Millennials can't understand the older cohorts who seem to be stuck in their jobs and have no passion for their work, while older generations think that Millennials are lazy slackers who have no real work ethic. So, let's begin by identifying and defining each of the potential four generations that are currently working and then determine how this generation gap can be managed and lead to more successful business ventures.

me! me! me!

Beginning with the oldest members of the workforce, let's take a look at the Silent Generation. The Silent Generation are people who were born between 1927 and 1945. They began working in a time when businesses were bureaucratic and hierarchical. That means that any individual person in the workplace was taught to 'stay in their lane,' so to speak. Managers made all of the decisions and employees under them were expected to do as they were told - without asking very many questions or challenging the status quo. Hierarchy was the key. Each person knew their place and was eager to take steps to move up the corporate ladder. Managers were responsible for coming up with ideas, while workers were responsible for making those ideas come to life. Think back to the example of IBM from earlier in Chapter Three - and for those of us who enjoy historical period dramas, consider the early seasons of the AMC popular drama "Mad Men." At IBM, the corporate culture was very much what the Silent Generation expects. Everyone was serious about their work, spent long hours in the office trying to 'get ahead,' and those in the lower ranks were discouraged from coming up with creative and innovative ideas. During this time, workers were rewarded for being a team player, not for going out on their own and shaking things up. There was little room for a divergent thinker or a visionary in this kind of corporate culture, which was pervasive in the United States. The majority of the Silent Generation believed in getting a job, working hard, and making enough money to own a small home in the "nice part of town," and take care of their families. Members of this generation were, therefore, a little more ambitious as they entered the workplace. However, because the workplace of the Silent Generation was one in which women and people of color had limited opportunities and many barriers to face, it was the most different from the workplace of today.

So, members of the Silent Generation will likely be less excited than their younger counterparts about change – of any kind. They like to stick to what works and that means putting your head down and getting the job done. Loyalty is extremely important to them, so they will not easily understand the need to move on and upward that many younger people have. On the other hand, this exposure to such a strict corporate culture makes members of the Silent Generation excellent mentors. They are a wealth of knowledge and have worked carefully and through great difficulty to get where they are today. As mentors and leaders, members of the Silent Generation are a relatively untapped resource in the workplace, as many of them are dismissed for having a way of doing things that just doesn't match up with how things are done today.

However, if younger generations would take the time to learn from the Silent Generation, they would find eager listeners and solid "workhorses."

The next oldest generation that remains well represented in the current American workplace is the Baby Boomers. Born between 1946 and 1964, this generation is the largest of the generations, by number – even though Millennials are now the largest generation currently in the workforce today. Baby Boomers began working in a corporate culture that was not unlike that of the Silent Generation. They are accustomed, however, to fierce competition for positions. This means that they like to work hard; in fact, they are often called 'workaholics' because of their level of dedication to any job. Also, Baby Boomers are the most likely generation to define themselves as individuals by what job they hold. You may find that Baby Boomers have difficulty separating, for example, who they are with what they do.

me! me! me!

A certain prestige is connected to higher level positions in the Baby Boomer mind – one that Gen Xers and Millennials have a hard time understanding. Younger generations do not define themselves by their position or their career the way that Baby Boomers do.

You've likely heard the phrase "Thank God It's Friday." For Baby Boomers, it has often been said that their work ethic can be defined by a different, but similar phrase: "Thank God It's Monday." This is how dedicated and connected to their work Baby Boomers are. In addition, the corporate culture in which Baby Boomers began working was extremely competitive. For the Silent Generation, once a person entered the workplace, a company or business would reward loyalty with loyalty – it was easy to remain in one job until retirement and to reap the benefits of having remained with one company for all of one's working life. Baby Boomers had a different experience altogether. It was more difficult for them to maintain the same position with the same company. Downsizing and corporate shakeups were common in the Baby Boomers' work experience, so they may have been forced to take a number of jobs with a few different companies just to get ahead or to keep their families afloat financially.

However, Boomers are also all about values and ethics. They are, perhaps, the most ethical and values-centered generation of the four discussed here. This makes them valuable resources, not only for their varied and interesting work experiences, but also for their insistence on doing things in an ethical way. After the scandals of the early 2000s, like Enron and Arthur Anderson, ethics and values have become imprinted into corporate culture in a way that they had never been before. Even the federal government now takes into consideration whether or not an "ethics and compliance" program is in place at a particular business or corporation before determining how to punish them for misconduct. Before, the language in the law only spoke of 'compliance;' now it refers to ethics as well. Baby Boomers understand this need for ethics and values and hold it dear.

Generation X is, perhaps, the most difficult of these four generations to define or 'pin down.' There is even disagreement among scholars about where this generation officially ends. Most people place the first year of birth at 1965, but where this generation ends is harder to say. Some say that it ends as early as 1976, while others say that it ended in 1981. Whatever the case, Gen Xers are the second largest generation in the workforce - but they are very different from their parents and grandparents. For Gen Xers, corporate culture is something of which to be suspicious. In fact, Gen Xers are pretty much suspicious of everything connected to social norms or conformity. They detest being followers and are generally the most independent of all the generations discussed here. This is the generation, for example, that hates to be helped when they are shopping. They'd rather find things on their own, thank you very much.

Their overarching suspicion is understandable when we think of what was happening when Gen Xers were entering the workplace. They had already grown up watching workplace and political scandals being discussed on television. Some of them were old enough to remember President Nixon's resignation and the distrust that it brought with it. At the time, every leader they knew was lying, cheating, and failing. The response? Skepticism. About everything.

This means that Gen Xers are also very skeptical about their work life. A job is just a job to a Gen-Xer; it is a stepping-stone in a series of commitments that will lead to eventual success. Gen Xers are under no illusions about corporate loyalty or big institutions – they distrust them both. Gen Xers were also the first generation to grow up in non-traditional households. Forty percent of their parents were divorced and, unlike the Silent Generation and the Baby Boomers, Gen Xers are likely to have had both parents in the workforce. They were the first generation of "latchkey" kids, letting themselves into their homes after school while they waited for one parent or another to return from work.

Gen Xers also grew up seeing how miserable it made their parents to work long hours and dedicate themselves fully to their jobs. This doesn't mean that Gen Xers have a terrible work ethic, only that they try very hard to create a balance between their work and home lives. Whereas Baby Boomers defined themselves entirely by the work that they did, Gen Xers are more likely to keep work and home life separate and to value their own identities over their work identities. Gen Xers, as skeptics, like to protect themselves – whether on a personal level or in the workplace. Additionally, Gen Xers work because they love what they do. They do not take jobs or assignments just because they are told to do so; they take them because they are passionate about them or about what their work will accomplish. As a group, Gen Xers are idealistic, desiring to change the world that they live in. They would rather work hard and get paid less in a particular job – if that job gives them the ability to help to make the world a better place. In fact, from 2000-2010, the "prime time" of Millennials entering the workforce, employment at non-profit organizations soared while employment in the for-profit arena declined. This trend may be due to the way that Millennials think about work – and how dedicated they are to making the world around them better.

Gen Xers, however, are also more laid back in their work practices than members of older generations.

me! me! me!

While they understand the value of getting a good job done, they are more likely to understand and accept younger generations. Gen Xers were rebels and outcasts as they came of age, so they understand the desire for innovation, creativity, divergent thinking, and non-conformity. In fact, Gen Xers are both the most and least likely allies for Millennials in the workplace. While Gen Xers value some Millennial traits, they have a hard time with anyone who they perceive to be dependent, unable to think for themselves, unfocused, or distracted.

Lastly, of course, is the Millennial generation. It is generally accepted that Millennials were born after 1982. Unlike Gen-Xer latchkey kids, Millennials grew up in a world where technology reigned, parental supervision was tight, and their schedules were chock full of a variety of after school and weekend activities – all overseen by adults. For this reason, among others, Millennials have a hard time being independent and may also have difficulty addressing conflict – both in their personal lives and in the workplace.

Remember, too, that Millennials were affected by at least two major occurrences that caused their worldview to differ from generations that came before them. First, they witnessed the tech rise – and subsequent fall – in the 1990s and early 2000s. Witnessing this, Millennials got the impression that they needed to have a secure job, not a job that they love. So, many Millennials enter college classrooms with one goal in mind: getting a steady job with a steady income. They have a hard time trading financial security for something that they are passionate about. This does not mean that Millennials cannot be passionate about their jobs. As we have seen, one quality that makes transformative narcissists good leaders is their ability to spread their passion for their work to others, to make others share in their vision. Yet, still, Millennials that enter the workforce today are very concerned about obtaining work in fields like health care because of the job security that they afford. Second, Millennials were still young when the terrorist attacks on the Twin Towers occurred on September 11, 2001. After seeing image after image of firefighters, nurses, and EMTs rifling through the wreckage of the aftermath of 9/11, Millennials view these professions as important and heroic.

This view of heroism might be the reason that Millennials are also community-oriented. Perhaps they are more community oriented than the Silent Generation and the Baby Boomers. They want to know that their profession makes a difference, like Gen Xers, but are usually unwilling to trade financial security for their dreams.

Millennials are true collaborators in the workplace. They are the first generation to grow up in what many people refer to as the "age of technology." That means that they were first to be exposed to technology – and social media – in any meaningful way. Perhaps one way to explain this is that Millennials have grown up in a world in which information is easily accessible. Think about it; because of the lack of current technology, the world moved a lot slower than it does now. Millennials grew up after that change had really occurred. If older generations wanted to conduct research or other work-related information-gathering, it took a long time to collect, process, and make data understandable and transferrable. Now, Millennials understand that this can be done with the click of a trackpad.

Understanding technology and the way that the world had become fast-paced is something that comes naturally to Millennials. It has also changed the way that we work. A change in workforce means a change in the culture of a workplace. Take, for example, the prevalence of social media in today's working world. Millennials are the first generation to truly be affected by the presence of social media – they understand it, use it, and are adept at mining it for advertising and client-building purposes. For older generations, this kind of technology is unfamiliar. Sure, Gen Xers were exposed to it in its older forms, but those were nothing like what we see today.

Additionally, this focus on social media and information-gathering has contributed to the narcissism of Millennials. Before the advent of social media, there was very little reason for people to share information about themselves with the world. This kind of sharing was limited to close friends and people that you knew in real life. Now, social media creates a strange kind of pressure. This pressure is to be perceived to have a "perfect," "normal," productive life as perceived by others. Social media has caused people to concentrate more on themselves and less on others, to become more self-centered and focused on their own lives. Millennials are caught up in this new way of thinking about the world – that everything is public, shared, and immediate. How could this fail to change the workplace – and make Millennials more narcissistic?

The obvious differences in worldview of each of the four generations defined here make for an interesting mix in any workplace. Generational affects are meaningful and if we understand them properly, we can create a workplace in which each generation can work successfully with the others. This is not, however, easy.

Think of the relationships that exist between parents, guardians, and children. Growing up, children learn from their parents and/or guardians. Parents and guardians teach lessons that they themselves may not even know they are passing on. However, once a child reaches a certain age, they yearn to differentiate themselves from how their parents or guardians think and act. This is a good thing. If children and their parents/guardians thought enough alike, perhaps children would never leave their homes and strike out on their own. So, it is normal for generations to disagree, to push back upon one another, and to have competing worldviews. This is just the way things are. The situation becomes more difficult when members of several different generations – all with different experiences, attitudes, values, ethical beliefs, morals, and views – have to work together in harmony to create a successful business or workplace culture.

We know that corporate culture can have important effects on all stakeholders in a corporation or business. Corporate culture often strives to be monolithic and unchanging. The founder or founders of a particular corporation or business may have one view of how that business or corporation ought to be run. However, corporate culture *must* change – and often – in order to keep up with the times. It may move at the speed of an iceberg, but it moves. Corporate cultures are also known to affect individuals – more than an individual can affect corporate culture. In a workplace that is inclusive of many different points of view, there may be gaps in understanding between generations that causes problems and issues. The way to avoid these problems and issues is through understanding.

In fact, these 'generation gaps' may be somewhat closed, or at least bridged, by understanding what strengths each generation has to offer. Put these strengths together, instead of considering them insurmountable and you will have a successful workplace team and a diverse corporate culture. There are many ways in which this could be accomplished, but, as mentioned above, members of the Silent Generation make great mentors, members of the Baby Boomers have varied and vast experiences, Gen Xers value independence and divergent thinking. While parents of Millennials have provided unprecedented protection and support for their children - to some degree fostering a very dependent relationship, they have also managed to raise a generation who is not fearful of risk and dancing to the beat of their own drum. Millennials are willing to take that 'once in a lifetime' opportunity and pursue paths that are considered high-risk all because they believe in it. There is a current struggle within this generation - on the one hand, financial security, on the other hand, the potential to change the world. I believe this comes from having a mix of Gen Xers and Baby Boomers as parents. Millennials have compiled mixed traits from their parents, social media, and cultural norms, which has them a little all over the place.

Danielle Shepherd

Because Millennials are the first generation to have truly grown up with technology, social media, and other strong cultural forces, they are better prepared to make a positive impact in the current workplace environment. All of that diverse experience and knowledge can be put to use – if only the generations could understand one another better. One way that older generations could more positively view Millennials is through the positive, productive, and transformational leadership they are capable of providing. Transformational leadership is the kind of leadership that is needed in this new and ever-changing work world – and Millennials are the future of transformational leadership.

Chapter Five

A New Now:

Leadership that Transforms

We all know that the world is continually changing. Over the past forty or fifty years, it has changed more quickly than anyone thought possible. Besides paying close attention to generational effects in the workplace, we also need to determine what kind of leadership will best fit this new and changing world. We need great leaders – and transformative narcissists may be the answer. We live in the present, but a "new now" is on the way and we need leadership that transforms to see us through.

In my work on transformative narcissism, I discovered that transformative narcissism was really a leadership personality characteristic – and that narcissism was more than a personality disorder. Some researchers have even said that narcissism is really a trait associated with normal personalities, that it is a common trait found in various types of leaders around the world. In fact, there are a number of narcissistic leaders who have achieved things that are considered "great." In general, what I've found is that society depends on narcissists to accomplish what was once unthinkable. Alexander the Great, Gaius Julius Caesar Augustus Germanicus, Abraham Lincoln, Henry Ford, John D. Rockefeller, Bill Clinton, Steve Jobs, and Bill Gates are just a few productive narcissists who have proven to be great leaders. Even Adolf Hitler and Joseph Stalin were effective leaders, though their visions for the world were dangerous ones.

All of the leaders mentioned above have three things in common. First, they were or are narcissists.

me! me! me!

Second, each was able to accomplish the unthinkable. Third, they are or were considered some of the most capable leaders in history. Setting aside the fact that some of these leaders' accomplishments were deplorable, they still attracted a vast following and were able to reach goals that those before them failed to reach – or never even attempted to reach. They all brought to life visions that have changed the world and challenged the rules of the societies they lived in. They also exhibited narcissistic characteristics. Yet, they led their followers on a journey that resulted in greatness. This is the very making of a transformative narcissist. The term 'narcissist' is used to describe activities, behaviors, and experiences that serve to maintain or enhance a grandiose, yet exposed sense of self.

Many different people have defined leadership in many different ways. There are charismatic leaders, transformational leaders, transactional leaders, visionary leadership, ethical leadership, and self-leadership. Many of these styles of leadership have been researched thoroughly. What was found is that each style is more complex and multi-layered than previously thought. Research shows that transformational leadership has a number of different elements. Transformational leadership is, in fact, among the types of leadership that have been found to be most effective in changing organizations and having a significant effect on its followers. Narcissism, according to many studies of leadership, is a characteristic of several leadership styles. In particular, narcissism is a trait that Millennial transformational leaders possess.

It is only in recent years that narcissism has been linked to leadership. We already know that leadership is a process in which a single individual influences a group of individuals to achieve a common goal or task. That is the basic definition of any kind of leadership. However, it can also mean bringing together groups of people who have many different abilities, gifts, and skills to achieve certain objectives and goals. We can draw two conclusions from these ideas about leadership. First, it is clear that researchers and scholars have trouble agreeing on what leadership truly is. Second, the actual word "leadership" is fairly new. As a matter of fact, the term "leadership" was not used until after the twentieth century and was not officially studied until after World War II. One set of researchers even defined over 1,000 constructs and 92 different categories of leadership. Now, that's quite a number of different ways in which to lead!

So, you can see, the concept of leadership and what we know about it has evolved over the years. To say the least, leadership has been studied from many angles. We now know that there are certain connections between some personality traits and different kinds of leadership. Each leadership style that is studied has added to the definitions and meanings of the word. Again, the choices are staggering. Leadership styles include: transformational, visionary, authentic, servant, charismatic, transactional, laissez-faire, and ethical. Leadership styles vary as widely as the definitions of leadership itself. The leadership styles mentioned above have all been studied – from many different perspectives. Some have criticized these styles, while others have suggested that they are positive. Transformational leadership, however, is among those leadership styles that are generally considered 'good.' Transformational leadership is considered to be positive or 'good' because people consider transformational leaders to be 'good' people – people who are morally just.

Transformational leaders encourage a change in the goals of their followers. New goals can then be seen as more important, or 'higher priority' than previous goals. Once a transformational leader transforms the goals of his or her followers, the new goals represent the interests of everyone – leaders and followers together. Transformational leaders are often found to have self-confidence, self-determination, and self-control. They are able, not only to lead others, but to *inspire* them. This is an important difference. Many leaders can be merely ethical, just, or good. Not many leaders are able to take that goodness, ethicality, and justice and transform the workplace or the world. On the other hand, if a leader is not perceived to be ethical, just, and good, they are unlikely to be transformational leaders. People often refuse to follow someone that they believe to be bad, unethical, or unjust. Goodness, ethicality, and justice legitimize the transformational leader's goals and makes others feel good about following them. When transformational leaders make an impact on the members of an organization or group, it is thus likely to be positive.

People have different opinions about the "power" of transformational leaders. Some will say that transformational leaders are limited by their narcissistic characteristics, that such leaders have fantasies about getting more power and success – and are willing to go to extremes to get them. Transformational leaders bear a good deal of responsibility on their backs. They have the power and influence to change the goals of their followers, but they can use this power either to do good deeds or to do things that present moral challenges (like Adolf Hitler). But, research shows that the 'good' and 'bad' powers of transformational leaders are separate. Leaders, who emulate past luminaries like Dr. Martin Luther King, Jr., use their power and influence for good, whereas others use their powers for more negative purposes.

me! me! me!

Transformational leadership is different, too, from transactional leadership. This was discovered in the late 1970s. Both are basic types of leadership, but they differ in the way that they manifest themselves. Since that time, other kinds of leadership have been added to what is now a kind of continuum of leadership – bookended by transformational and transactional leadership on either end. More than this, transformational leadership and transactional leadership are often viewed as a one way highway, where transformational leadership is viewed as 'best' (in the sense of resulting in "good") and can involve transactional leadership, while transactional leadership is considered 'limited' (in the sense that it does not go beyond transactional exchanges). Maybe this is because transactional leadership is marked by an exchange between leader and follower(s) that is mutually beneficial. In transactional leadership, this exchange is dependent on how well the follower both obeys and meets the expectations of the leader. Transactional leaders often have their own agenda – and they pursue it without taking other people into consideration. Transformational leadership, on the other hand, requires that the leader and follower share a goal, even though that goal is the leader's own vision, and work together toward it. A transformational leader does, in fact, care about other people and takes them into consideration.

If leadership is about getting followers to embrace a higher purpose beyond their own self-interest, then transformational leadership does this very well. Transformational leadership is visible when a leader is able to encourage his or her followers to work, encourages a view from a new perspective, tells followers about his or her mission or vision, helps followers discover self-awareness and potential, and encourages followers to look past their own self-interest to what is in the best interest of the group or organization. This is what is known as the "Four I's:" idealized influence (behaviors and attributes), inspirational motivation, intellectual stimulation, and individualized consideration. Let's take a look at each of these I's individually.

The first of these is *idealized influence.* This kind of influence requires a transformational leader to be a role model. When that transformational leader becomes a role model, he or she gains the respect, admiration, and trust from their followers. If a transformational leader wishes to do this, he or she must first get rid of any anxiety that they might have. When a person is free from anxiety, their mind is allowed to flow freely, making it easier for them to gain followers through their ease, painting a positive picture of themselves in the meantime. As mentioned before, a transformational leader must also behave in such a way that other people see him as having high ethical standards and a solid moral code. If a transformational leader is able to be persistent, determined, and willing to take risks, he will find that people will follow him. Why? Because followers want to be just like their leaders – when they perceive that their leaders are good people who will lead them well.

The second of the I's is *inspirational motivation.* With inspirational motivation, a transformational leader motivates people by helping them find meaning and challenge in their work. People need to believe that their work is meaningful and they need to be challenged. Otherwise, they will become bored and will not be invested in the business, corporation, or group. The transformational leader must also show enthusiasm and a positive attitude – all while encouraging "team work." A successful transformational leader is able to communicate effectively with his or her followers and help them to commit to a shared vision. Also, when a transformational leader is in charge, followers know what is expected of them and are therefore able to follow through in helping the leader to fulfill his or her vision.

The third of the I's is *intellectual stimulation*. This "I" calls for transformational leaders to be creative and innovative in approaching normal, daily tasks with a "fresh pair of eyes." Transformational leaders encourage creativity and are not afraid to listen to the opinions and ideas of their followers. To this end, opinions and ideas that followers suggest that go against what the transformational leader believes are not publicly criticized, but readily accepted as a different and important perspective.

Finally, the fourth "I" is *individualized consideration.* Individualized consideration happens effectively when the transformational leader acts as a mentor or coach and treats his or her followers like unique individuals. A good transformational leader will help individuals to achieve and to grow. If such a leader displays behavior that shows understanding and encourages individualism, he or she will be successful. Transformational leaders that are effective will listen to their individual followers and delegate tasks in such a way that they develop more followers. Unlike transactional leadership (in which there is a one-way exchange from leader to follower), in transformational leadership a two-way exchange is encouraged. When we take each of these four "I's" into consideration, we see that they require a leader to move beyond basic leadership models. They also extend the organization's best interest as an extension of individual interests.

Transformative narcissism shares a number of similarities with transformational leadership – the kind of leadership that we need in the "new now."

me! me! me!

Transformative narcissists, like transformational leaders, are internally motivated and are able to push others, toward a collective goal or vision. A transformative narcissist does not necessarily follow the four I's described above, but he or she does share similar characteristics with transformational leaders.

In fact, there is a strong relationship between the four I's and the productive aspects of productive narcissism, which is crucial to the makeup of transformative narcissism. Let me explain. Things like "idealized influence" and other good things like self-development both mean that a leader has to be a role model – or at least act like one. If a leader behaves like a role model, then followers will want to copy his or her behavior. "Idealized motivation" and the "vision" of productive narcissists are also similar. They both require a person to strive to communicate their goals – and to get people to share these goals and help bring them to life. A commitment toward a shared vision is important here. "Intellectual stimulation" and the productive narcissist's particular brand of systematic thinking help their followers to be innovative and creative while "individual consideration" and the productive narcissist's sense of caring require these leaders to listen to and focus on the needs of their followers. In other words, the four "I's" and the positive aspects of productive narcissism line up quite nicely, especially when it comes to engaging followers.

A transformative narcissist puts forth a good deal of effort to inspire his or her followers. They want to gain the admiration and trust of their followers - and to get them to share their vision for the future. Transformational leadership focuses on the development and wellbeing of individual employees or followers. Transformative narcissists are worried about using whatever resources they need - and are available to them – in order to bring their vision to life. From this transformational leadership, visionary leadership can happen. Visionary leaders and transformative narcissists also have a good bit in common with one another. Visionary leadership is a kind of transformational leadership.

So, what have we learned? We have learned that members of the Millennial generation embody transformative narcissism, which makes them leaders who allow the passion that they have for their vision to help them lead others. They are especially good at leading others through difficult situations, like times of rapid social and economic change. Currently, many societies around the globe are continuously evolving. Sometimes, they evolve too quickly for us to "catch up" or to truly be successful as organizations or groups. The world economy, too, is rapidly changing – and shows no signs of stopping. Leadership, the right kind of leadership, is more important now than ever before in history. It must evolve to meet the needs and demands of followers within organizations. Otherwise, it will be difficult for any business, organization, or group to maintain a successful lead in the societies in which they operate. True vision, and the promise of real progress, will encourage followers to move toward a collective goal – one that they hold just as dear as their transformational leaders.

This is an important trend to recognize since research shows that narcissistic characteristics are becoming more pronounced in younger generations. This suggests that we need to take a good, hard look at the ways in which transformative narcissism can help us to understand what the future may bring. Transformative narcissism, in fact, offers a unique perspective about future leaders and leadership. It can

easily be implemented into current leadership styles –
and folded into them.

This is where my research comes in. In order to
better understand the connections between
transformational leadership and productive narcissism, I
wanted to know whether individuals who were
productive narcissists could also be transformational
leaders. What I discovered was pretty amazing. There
does, in fact, seem to be a connection between people
who are productive narcissists and have a
transformational leadership style. This made good sense
to me, as I already knew how much the two have in
common. First, productive narcissism does exist – and
such qualities are strongly associated with leadership
and measurable through a questionnaire. In fact, it is an
interesting leadership style all on its own. The second
interesting result was finding out that narcissism can,

indeed, have a healthy form and could even be an essential part in normal human development.

The simple fact is that leadership is constantly evolving. The people who lead and those who are managed by leaders are always changing. The fact that productive narcissists have appeared in the workplace shows that there is a need for leaders to become progressive and to be open to changes in their style of leadership. As the workplace is now dominated by Millennials, now is the perfect time for transformative narcissism to be put into action.

Workplaces around the world have changed dramatically because of technological advancements. They have also changed because our idea of "work" has changed. We no longer have the same ways of thinking about defining "work" or about how work should be completed. Millennials are streaming into the workforce and they have raised concerns about old management practices and about workplace satisfaction. For a generation that has been identified as the most narcissistic generation in history, problem areas in management and leadership could be solved by transformative narcissists transforming the workplace. We need to know about narcissism in the workplace – and we need to know about it in this new now. Engagement with transformative narcissists in leadership positions will be a necessary thing in the future; it is even necessary now. We ought to break the stigma associated with narcissism and see the potential it can hold when rightfully balanced – a deep well of transformational and visionary leadership. In fact, one of the hidden gems of my study was that women are more likely to be transformative narcissists than men. This means that we need to look at narcissism in a whole new light – considering that men are more likely to be viewed as narcissists than women. Let's take a look at how female narcissists might change the world.

Chapter Six

Who Runs the World?

~~Boys~~? Girls!

It has long been thought that men are more likely to be narcissists than women. Because of gender and sex stereotypes that have existed since time immemorial, women are viewed to be gentler, kinder, and more considerate of others than their male counterparts. While it could be incorrect to generalize about either men or women here, it is interesting that the *perception* of women has not been that they are narcissists.

Think of all the different generations we discussed in the fourth chapter of this book. Certainly the Silent Generation had fewer women in the workforce than the other four generations mentioned. By the time the Baby Boomers were entering the workforce, women were a more common sight and were dominating positions in areas such as nursing and teaching. Gen-X women came along, and started their pursuit of dominating sectors such as the nonprofit world. With the path of development and growth 'blazed,' Millennial women are not only the most prevalent in higher education but their talent and perspectives are sought for positions all over the world. Even though the workplace has made substantial progress over the past 70 years, sexism, gender stereotypes, and glass ceilings remain significant concerns by professional women.

Why are women not viewed as possible narcissists? Are women capable of embodying narcissistic characteristics *and* becoming transformational leaders? Gender roles have made a significant shift over the last few decades and my research has raised the question of how many men and

me! me! me!

women have narcissistic personality characteristics and could, therefore, become transformational leaders. Are women more likely to be transformative narcissists than men? Let's first take a look at gender roles throughout the last one hundred years and how they have significantly changed.

One hundred years ago, things were different for both men and women across the globe. If we look only to the United States, we can see that we now take a lot of things for granted when it comes to sexual freedom, the equality of marriage, how labor is divided in the home space, and gender equality in general. Even as early as one hundred years ago, women were just beginning to fight for their reproductive, voting, and general rights as human persons. The U.S. Women's Movement was just getting started and women wanted their rightful, and equal, place among men. There is no doubt that, in the United States, we still live in a patriarchal culture. What this means is that men are still considered to be more important and privileged over women. If you are a woman and a member of a minority group, then things can still be very difficult for you. In fact, women in the U.S. still make only 80 cents for every dollar that a man makes – for minority women, this statistic is actually less. Living in a society that is still primarily ruled by men also means that women remain "second-class citizens" with fewer advantages than men – especially in the workplace.

One hundred years ago, it was quite rare for a woman to work outside of the home, unless she was working as a maid or as some other kind of domestic servant. This all changed with World War I. Because all of the able-bodied men were out fighting the war, women were able to enter into professions and roles from which they normally would have been barred. And women did a great job! They were just as good at the jobs in which they replaced men during the First World War as the men were. But, when the men came home and the war was over, women went back to their domestic sphere. They reared children, took care of the home, and made certain that everything in the household operated smoothly. Then, during World War II, the same thing happened again. Women were allowed to take jobs outside of the home that they would not normally have had access to. The iconic image of a woman such as this is "Rosie the Riveter," a strong-looking woman working in a factory while the men are away. The phrase "We can do it!" is emblazoned over her head and this piece of advertising was meant to encourage women to do just that - jobs that men normally did.

The unintended result of the need for women to leave the home and take men's place in the workplace during the First and Second World Wars was that women found that they enjoyed leaving and working outside of their homes. They had gotten a taste of freedom and weren't likely to forget it any time soon. These first steps toward gender equality led women to fight through the extremely conservative decade that the 1950s were and, eventually, to find their own power in the 1960s during the sexual revolution that was also a cultural revolution.

So, women have come quite a long way in their search for equality and understanding. However, narcissism is still normally associated with men. When you think of a narcissist, even the leaders that were mentioned earlier in this book, your mind likely turns to an image of a man. But, women can be narcissists too. True narcissism is a set of personality traits, after all, and it cannot therefore be gender-specific.

Many people would find it difficult to believe that women, too, can be narcissists. Maybe women are subtler at displaying these particular characteristics or maybe some of them are mistaken for being simply self-confident. However, we do know that if women are actually more likely to embody narcissism and transformational leadership than men (as my research shows), then wouldn't they make transformative narcissists? Again, we think of egotism and smugness, we tend to think of these things, not as narcissistic characteristics, but *male* characteristics. This is, perhaps, one of the most common ideas about narcissism – that it is *only* a male thing. Although female narcissists may reveal themselves differently than male narcissists, female narcissists do exist.

It used to be the case, not that long ago, that 75% of people diagnosed with narcissistic personality disorder were male. Additionally, although only 15% of college students in the early 1980s had high scores on the Narcissistic Personality Inventory survey, that number has jumped to 25%. Some scholars say that this increase in the number of narcissists is due to there being a larger number of narcissistic women. Why are there more narcissistic women than there were before? Many would say that this is because Millennials have been parented a particular way. I've already mentioned that Millennials are perceived to be entitled. Some say this is because their parents catered to them, did everything for them, allowed them to make decisions that adults usually make – like what's for dinner. While every generation up through Gen-X were told things like "Because I said so" or "Just do as you're told," the parents of Millennials have taught them that the world should cater to them – because their parents catered to them. Whether this is true for Millennials across the board is irrelevant. For the most part, the way that parents treated Millennials did have a huge effect on their behavior as adults. In a study done by Twenge and

Campbell, 30% of students admitted that they thought that they should earn high grades in their college classes simply for attending class – not for doing the actual work. This is a very different attitude toward education than Millennials' parents and grandparents have and had.

Also, because of the increased freedom and opportunities for women in the United States in general, Millennial women have had more access to education and jobs than their counterparts in older generations. Perhaps the increase in the number of female narcissists simply has to do with more women being in college and in the workforce. In today's world, women and men are also encouraged to live their lives much more publicly. The invention of social media sites like Facebook and Twitter encourage narcissistic tendencies. What self-respecting Millennial doesn't have a high number of selfies posted to their social media accounts? Also, the fascination with celebrities and their lives has grown over the years – teaching younger people that dysfunction and narcissism is the norm.

It isn't easy to find an example of a female narcissist – we are so accustomed to looking for them in the wrong places. We can think of female characters from movies (like Natalie Portman in "Black Swan" and Meryl Streep in "The Devil Wears Prada"), but female narcissists are all around us. You know women who are narcissists in the sense of having narcissistic personality disorder. They are the women who dress provocatively for attention, never admit when they are wrong, put themselves before anyone else, and make sure to wear designer clothes. She is more likely than other women to have breast augmentation surgery and plastic surgery in general. Appearances matter to her, even if she has to go broke buying the things she wants and neglecting the things she needs. A female narcissist will believe that she is the most beautiful person on the planet – even if she is no better looking than the average person. She is very materialistic and competitive, thinking that she is better and smarter than everyone else. She is a terrible listener and talks about herself constantly, even directing conversation toward the events in her life at the expense of others. She will be likely to put her friends down constantly and lie just to suit her own purposes. Of course, she'll never admit that she is that manipulative and dishonest because nothing is ever her fault. This list of characteristics and behaviors is not to say that every girl who is a terrible listener, talks about themselves constantly, or gets plastic surgery is a narcissist – instead it is to showcase a number of behaviors that make up the typical parts of a narcissistic personality, and can be applied across genders.

We can easily recognize the negative traits that a female narcissist might possess. The traits and actions mentioned above are examples of traditional narcissistic behaviors. They really aren't very different than the ones that male narcissists display. The differences between men and women narcissists become apparent when we look at women as transformative narcissists. Men keep many of the traditional negative traits even when they are transformative narcissists, but women who are transformative narcissists modify their behavior in order to promote their transformational side and hide their narcissistic side, because of this their narcissism will be that much harder to detect. Productively, she will be a master manipulator. She will appear empathetic even if she lacks empathy. She will be an excellent listener [but not in the traditional sense] only for information that is useful to obtain her vision and goals. Her transformational leader persona will act as her face and reputation, while her narcissistic personality is what drives her. The people closest to her will know that her vision, passion, and ambition is authentic, but it comes at a price. Her personality is equally balanced between transformational and productively narcissistic. The very reason as to why women are not 'normally' perceived as narcissists is because they are better at hiding it and better at productively balancing the negative aspects to be used for good, than men. Yet, as we have seen, narcissism doesn't always have to be negative – it can be healthy and productive. It can be the foundational ingredient for an advanced version of transformational leadership that can take the corporate and business worlds to the necessary next level.

It was really the "gem" of my study to find that my respondents were primarily female. I think it is clear that women can – and do – embody narcissistic characteristics and practice transformational leadership. If we look at women who "rule the world," we can see many examples of women who are both productive narcissists and transformational leaders. Michelle Obama, Hillary Clinton, Angela Merkel, and Ruth Bader Ginsberg are all women who have held top-level positions in the United States government and were able to effect big changes for the country because of their powerful positions. Here are some female transformational leaders that you may not have heard about.

First up is Lu Zhang, a graduate of Stanford University in materials science and engineering. After graduation, she sold her medical device startup company to open her own venture capital firm (NewGen Capital), which, by all accounts, is already very successful. When interviewed by Forbes Magazine, Zhang said that she doesn't like anyone to tell her what to do, that she likes challenges, and that she rises to every occasion. Clearly, this is a woman who has a vision, is capable of getting others to follow it, and has been successful due to her transformational leadership and productive narcissism. There are others, like Lexie Komisar founding member of IBM's Digital Innovation Lab, Whitney Wolfe (founder and Ceo) of Bumble, Lisy Kane of Girl Geek Academy whose goal is to teach 1 million women to get into tech and start their own startup by 2025, among many others

From what we already know about the connection between productive narcissists and transformational leadership, we can really begin to speculate what it would mean for women to be transformative narcissists. As leaders, it is necessary to maintain an open mind in order to establish a bridge between the new workforce, mainly Millennials, and the existing workforce. Because Millennials, and Millennial women, are currently taking over the workforce in large numbers, it is good to remember that this group will contain quite a few narcissists. Many of these narcissists will be productive ones, able to lead and get others to follow. To keep leadership effective, it is also important to understand all personality types – and genders – in the workplace. By learning more about the narcissistic personality and the prevalence of women who have this personality, current leaders can devise plans about how to create projects that encourage self-development and creativity in a team or group environment.

When you think about it, it's no wonder that the positive type of narcissism should be associated with women more than men. Women today are strong, creative, and empowered. Millennial women are unlikely to let very much get in their way. Whereas women in the Silent Generation, the Baby Boomers, and Gen-X actually witnessed women in their limited roles, Millennials are less likely to have had this experience. It's completely foreign to them to think that women can't do the same things as men.

me! me! me!

Women have fought hard for exactly this kind of freedom and equality over the years. Even though women are not yet equal as far as the U.S. Constitution goes (the Equal Rights Amendment has never been ratified), there is a distinctly American ideology that says we are all equal. However, this is not always the case. Take a look at the makeup of faculties in universities, for example. Women make up only 15% of all full professors. Access to equality is not the same for everyone.

There is a mindset that persists that women do not belong in power. We have the vote, so what more do we need? We have women members of Congress, but not as many as there are men. Millennials are changing these perceptions. Women, as a group, no longer feel tied to old images of what they should be. This freedom and equality has led to an increase in powerful, self-confident women who can rule the world if they choose!

Gender refers to the way in which all societies organize and define sexual difference. Gender systems are, in fact, everywhere - in classrooms, kitchens, ballparks, nursery schools, and all kinds of other places. Because so many human societies have built their own gender systems, we think in terms of gender systems instead of a singular gender. Gender expectations change over time - and through society. What is happening now is that women are finding themselves more powerful and strong than ever before. If a strong woman seems narcissistic, it is possible that she is just a divergent and creative thinker - a visionary capable of bringing the world that she hopes for to fruition.

Women have not been seen as capable of narcissism in the past because they were not in a position to prove otherwise to anyone. Millennials, and especially female Millennials who possess the traits of a transformative narcissist, now have the power to change the way that the world views women in the workplace. As we have seen, the history of women in the workplace is still very young. In other words, women have not had the opportunity to be part of the workforce (outside of the home) for a very long time. But, women have the same capability of being good leaders and gaining followers as men do.

When it comes to leadership, we must stop thinking of healthy kinds of narcissism as solely about men. Women, too, possess these traits – and are exhibiting them more and more as time goes on. Again, the traits we are talking about are not the negative ones associated with narcissistic personality disorder. Instead, they are the traits of a leader who can make significant changes in the way that we see things, in the way that the workplace operates and in the goals that it meets. We have already discovered that the "new now" will require leaders of a different kind than before.

Keeping up with the fast pace of technology, economic changes, and many other factors will mean having leaders that are up to the task. A good transformational leader will be able to do this - but a transformative narcissist will be able to excel at this task.

Women may definitely fall into this group. Not all women will be narcissists or transformative narcissists. However, those that are will make a huge impact on the corporation or business with which they are involved and on the world in general. Making a larger impact is what transformational leaders do. They are able, when others are not, to make significant leaps in innovation and creativity. Because they think differently than others, they are able to see things that others are blind too. It is not surprising that women, who were underrepresented in the workplace for so long, might have ideas and come up with innovations that no one else has before. If women remain controlled, reasonable, self-determined, and have a good sense of ethics, they will be able to have a positive impact on their followers, groups, and organization.

More than this, if we continue to take stereotypes into consideration, who better to be a transformational leader than a woman? Women are usually known for their skills in compromising, working in teams, and collaborating. But, that is not all that women can do. The world has changed – and the view that women have of themselves has changed. Women in younger generations, like the Millennials, are not as limited and bound by old traditions. They know that women can be successful and strong, that they can have a distinct vision and succeed at getting others to help them realize it. Female narcissists will be the group to keep an eye on in the coming years. If these narcissists of the younger generation are transformative narcissists, then they will be a force to be reckoned with when it comes to transformational leadership. Women have already managed to transform the world in positive ways – why not in the workplace? Yet, Millennials who are women are not the only ones who can change or "run" the world. As a group, Millennials are already fast becoming important, successful up and coming members of the workforce.

Chapter Seven

Future Vision:

Millennials Change the World

We've covered a lot of ground so far. Now, we know that there are healthy and productive types of narcissism that can make for better, transformational leaders. Also, we have learned that many Millennials have these kinds of 'good' narcissistic tendencies – especially Millennial women. But, what about Millennials makes me so sure that they are the generation that can change the world for the better? What makes them better leaders in the workplace and gives them the advantage over generations that came before them? Is it just that they will make better transformational leaders?

The simple answer to the above question is: "Yes!" Each generation, as we know, has a very specific worldview. Millennials are no different. All Millennials will not fall into the category or have all of the characteristics described in this chapter. Nor, will all Millennials have the necessary skillset to be leaders. However, the Millennial worldview is so different from that of previous generations that it may be the only one that can keep up with the changing times and help usher in what I have called the "new now." So, let's take a deeper look at how the Millennial worldview actually shows a great deal of promise, how it may help us to build a better world - together.

Everyone likes to complain about Millennials, but does anyone in older generations truly understand them? We know that people think that Millennials are lazy, entitled screen junkies who could care less about the world around them, still live with their parents, and don't want to work hard to make an honest living. Millennials, if we listen to critics, are a generation with high expectations, while providing little to no hard work or effort to be rewarded. Yet, there are some really great things about Millennials that will make them great leaders, qualities that will help them to change the world for the better. To clarify, we are not saying that all Millennials - but many and especially those with transformative narcissism leadership qualities - are included in this group.

First, as far as a career is concerned, they want one with meaning. Millennials want to know that whatever they are doing will have some kind of positive impact on the world around them. In fact, they are willing to change jobs as often as they need to in order to find that meaning in their work. If they feel that their work is not meaningful, they are likely to quit and take another job that gives them a sense of working toward something important.

This may seem strange to older generations, but it is a good thing about Millennials. Employees who love their job and find meaning in it are more likely to stick around, to contribute to the goals of the organization, and to be positive assets in the workplace. Just think - most people in older generations really dislike their jobs. How many people can you name who truly appreciate their work and find meaning in it? Millennials have learned from the experiences of other generations - they know that people have to work to make a living, but they want *more* than this and are willing to search for it until they find it.

For example, you'll notice that nearly every tech company that has popped up in recent years claims that they will "change the world" through whatever platform they are peddling. This is because the opportunity to change the world is appealing – especially to Millennials. They want to provide something valuable, whether that is a product or a service. They want to contribute their part and are, therefore, willing to take more responsibility for their contributions because they are personal contributions. Millennials, in short, are *invested* employees; they want to be a part of something bigger than themselves and will work hard to accomplish their goals. If everyone in the workplace was as invested as Millennials are, then organizations and businesses would thrive even more than they do today.

Second, Millennials are not easily fooled. They are suspicious, much like Gen-X, about governmental institutions and about advertising. Millennials were young when the stock market bottomed out in 2008 and, because of this, they are great at refusing to trust the information that they get, even from normally credible sources. They take everything with a grain of salt and are experienced consumers of information. Think of how Millennials have grown up in an age where information is readily accessible. If you want to know about something, Google it. Want to know what that song is on the radio, Shazam it. Want to know what other people are thinking about a particular topic? Scroll through Facebook for personal opinions.

Some have said that Millennials are not astute consumers of information – that they believe everything they read. Nothing could be further from the truth. Because they know that information and news comes to them from multiple, maybe suspicious, sources, they are more likely than older generations to be able to filter through all of the nonsense and get to the truth. This is a valuable skill in the current workplace and Millennials have it in spades.

It's true: this very ability to search through tons of information is exactly one of the reasons why

me! me! me!

Millennials get the bad reputation of being entitled. Why? Because they want to know how things really work. A Millennial wants to get to the heart of the matter – and quickly. They don't want to know *why* things are done the way that they are, they want to know *how* they can accomplish goals and set standards.

This attitude is often mistaken for entitlement. If, for example, a Millennial employee walks into their boss's office and says, "I want to become the CEO of this company," their older manager might think that they are brazenly trying to put people out of a job. Or, worse, that the Millennial in question thinks that they are better than everyone else and could get such a high-level position easily. What the Millennial is really asking, though, is "What can I do to advance my career? What does it take to become a CEO?" This could range from being a doctor to being a business owner. It's really one of the ways in which we decide what we will major in during our college years. It's also how we determine what jobs to take and which ones to apply for as a plan to get us to where we ultimately want to be.

It is in this way that Millennials are often misunderstood. What is interpreted as entitlement might really be a search for transparency. They want to have access to all the information in a particular business. Again, this makes sense as they have come of age in a world where information is easily accessible to them. That isn't always the case in the working world. Sometimes, information cannot be shared with new employees (for various reasons). Millennials do not understand this and will be confused by what they interpret as a lack of access to information that they need.

This means that Millennials also like a lot of feedback. They need it. They want it in order to become better at their jobs and to advance as quickly as they can. Remember, Millennials know that the world we live in is constantly changing. They've seen quite a number of big changes in the world economy, technological advancements, and the societies in which they live. Millennials, then, perceive the world to be fragile. If you've ever wondered why you don't get it when a Millennial co-worker sends you a meme that makes no sense to you, it's because Millennials have responded to the constantly changing world by embracing absurdity. Much in the world is absurd to a Millennial – except those things that are valuable in helping to improve it. In fact, it is *because* they perceive the world as absurd that they want to change it in the first place.

Another thing that is really great about Millennials is that they have never lived in a world in which diversity was not the norm. To Millennials, diversity isn't even a question – it just exists. Recall that, for Baby Boomers, 90% of the population of the United States was white. Now, that percentage is dropping continuously every year. Remember, too, that there were far fewer women in the workplace before the Millennials entered into the workforce. The Silent Generation and Baby Boomers were less exposed to homosexuality, and speaking or openly acknowledging being gay was taboo. Gen Xers became a bit more aware of sexuality that did not fit into nice, neat categories.

So, whether we ask about race, gender, sexuality, or ethnicity, Millennials have grown up in a much more diverse world than generations that came before them. This puts them at a distinct advantage. Not only are they far less likely to discriminate against others, but they are also highly aware of remaining inclusive. When they look at their colleagues, or followers, they see *individual people*. This makes them much more likely to have success working in teams – and understanding the needs of each individual team member. When it comes to being a transformational leader, this skill is invaluable. And, for Millennials, this isn't even a skill; it's the status quo.

It is the mark of a good transformational leader that he or she can get other people to share in their vision for an organization. Who better than Millennials, as an inclusive group that understands diversity as the norm, to lead current and future organizations? For Millennials, diversity means cooperation and collaboration. In the workplace, current and future leaders need to have this understanding. In Millennials, this understanding is built into their worldview already. Understanding does not need to be taught to a Millennial – it's already just the way things are.

Another valuable part of the Millennial worldview is that they are independent and self-reliant. They have learned, much more than their Gen-X counterparts that they cannot depend on the stability of the societies that they live in. Millennials are deeply skeptical about relying on anyone to get things done. In fact, they would much rather rely on themselves to change the world.

Ask a Millennial to perform a task and they are less likely to delegate it to others. They believe that no one can get the job done as well as they can, so they take responsibility for it themselves. This particular trait fits in perfectly with my findings that Millennials have more narcissistic traits than previous generations. While self-reliance is not exactly the same thing as narcissism, a transformative narcissist will know that working as a team sometimes means leading that team. If the team cannot accomplish what needs to be done, then a Millennial will take that responsibility upon themselves. Again, not every Millennial you encounter will do this, but those who have transformative narcissism traits and a high level of transformational leadership traits will stand out among the rest, displaying strength and great leadership capabilities.

Millennials, in other words, share the strong belief that it is up to them to change the world – if it is to be changed at all. They have seen governmental systems fail to do this. Just take into consideration the recent protests concerning gun violence. When, in February of 2018, 17 students were killed at Marjory Stoneman Douglas High School in Parkland, Florida many people thought that this was just another tragic school shooting incident. However, the members of an even younger generation than the Millennials – Gen-Z, the most recent identifiable generation, spoke out. These young people have effected great change in the world simply by standing up and using their voices. The fact that they have had success in making their voices heard is really an extension of the Millennial push to take personal responsibility for changing the world. As the generations progress and change, we can expect to see more and more young people losing faith in business and governmental systems – and having more faith in themselves to effect real change.

This is, perhaps, another good point to make. Although we haven't gone into great detail on the generation after the Millennials, those individuals are coming of age and entering the workforce as we speak. The oldest members of the post-Millennials are between 18 to 23 years of age (where Generation Z begins is still being figured out by experts). Their parents are Gen Xers. For the first time in history, we already have *five* generations in the workplace – and Millennials are far better equipped to understand members of Gen-Z and to lead them in business. Leadership in this case is more prevalent than ever, since some experts are estimating that by 2020 around 70% of the workplace will be made-up of Millennials and Gen Z employees. Gen-Z was born *after* the Internet became a common thing. They are also the largest generation so far, outnumbering both Baby Boomers and Millennials. Who will lead this up-and-coming generation – a generation that is defined by a lack of faith in the "American Dream," has always lived in a time that the United States was at war with terrorism, and an even more striking level of independence than Gen Xers or Millennials?

It will be up to transformative narcissists to lead the charge into the "new now." Millennials, more than any other previous generation, also find feedback very important. They want to know how they are doing and they want to know as soon as possible. Because they underestimate the value of experience, many Millennials will be perceived to be arrogant or entitled. However, this perceived arrogance is difficult to prove when most Millennials want to know how things are currently working – and how they can be made better. That isn't arrogance; that's a desire to succeed, perform, and change things for the better.

Millennials want to see things immediately. They are impatient to know whether their work is good – and whether it is making a difference to the organization or business by which they are employed. In fact, what is often perceived as narcissism on a Millennial's part may be a simple desire to "fix" what's wrong. Unfortunately, older generations take offense to a desire to fix what is "broken." There has been a long-standing tradition of sweeping things under the rug and limiting effectiveness in the workplace – a tradition that many would like to see remain the same, but one that will not work for the two new generations who will soon dominate the workplace. In the "new now," the qualities that Millennials possess will be in great demand. What we need now, more than ever, are effective leaders who can make significant changes in the world - and the workplace.

Right now, Millennials are the best positioned to take on this new leadership role. In fact, Millennials are often called by other names - and some of them are telling. Sometimes they are referred to as "Generation Y," "Gen Why?," "Gen Next," "Baby Boomlets," "Echo Boomers," the MyPod generation, "Generation Waking Up," and the "Boomerang Generation." Most significantly, however, they are often referred to as "Generation Now." Why is this the case? It is because they don't have a lot of patience for the way things are and seek to change them immediately.

As the idea of transformational leadership suggests, transformational leaders *cause great change.* This change is always for the better, because it involves a very clear vision on the part of the leader and the ability of the leader to involve everyone around them in implementing their plan. The current state of the workforce in the United States is such that the old ways need to be abandoned in favor of strategies that will lead us to the next great thing. With Millennials at the helm of businesses and organizations, this change will happen – and it will be a positive change. Older generations may struggle with understanding this new era of leadership, and some may down-right dislike it, but the reality is as it has always been – the young will inherit the earth, and at some point, it will be what we make of it. While it is true that Millennials are impatient, it is also true that Millennials are willing to avoid confrontation and wait till our time comes in the formal workplace. But in the meantime Millennials know and understand their importance and other ways to have a significant impact on the way that business is done. Just look at the major changes in the last five years in marketing, news, and communication. The impact of

me! me! me!

Millennials is significant. We can just look at Kylie Jenner and how she made Snapchat lose a billion dollars in 24 hours or the other billion that Snapchat lost due to Rhianna's complaints.

While each generation that is currently in the workforce has their own part to play, like that of mentors and persons with a good deal of experience to draw upon, Millennials are tough, self-reliant, and self-starters. They are not at all the lazy, screen-obsessed kids that the older generations like to think they are. Millennials can process information at high rates of speed, develop a vision, and with self-confidence move themselves and others toward reaching important goals. Transformative narcissists do not suffer from self-doubt, they can really get things done in a way that others cannot. Many Millennials possess these traits, which – up until recently – were considered negative. What we need to do is to *grow* Millennials, give them the challenges and opportunities that they need in order to support their work.

If you are a Millennial, then you already know that what has been written here is true. You know that you are not lazy, but lack challenges. You know that it's frustrating when you work in a place that keeps information from you for seemingly ridiculous reasons. You know the power that you hold within you to make important and radical changes will end in making the world a better place. The dream that you have is a world in which businesses and organizations can come together, work swiftly and collaboratively, and deliver the services and goods that are needed. You also know that you have many capabilities – and that your self-confidence is not arrogance, but a desire to simply get things done the right way and to lead others to help you in attaining your goals.

me! me! me!

If you are not a Millennial, then you should take a closer look at what Millennials are currently accomplishing. Take the time to sit with your Millennial colleagues. Talk to them and find out what it is that they really want. I'll bet that you will be surprised at their answers. Likely, you will find willing employees and managers who are simply misunderstood. They can't understand why things have to be done a certain way because they are used to thinking in divergent ways. Let them be creative. Mold them, not in your image, but with the understanding that your experience is important, too. If you understand things from their perspective, instead of criticizing them and throwing your hands in the air, then they will not disappoint you. All Millennials want, when it comes to the workplace, is to feel valued and respected. And isn't this what we all want? Whether you are a member of the Silent Generation, a Baby Boomer who had to struggle, an independent-minded

Gen-Xer who wants work/life balance, or a Millennial striving to understand their older co-workers or followers, understanding one another is the key to real success.

Millennials can't change the world on their own. They desperately want to, but they will need the advice and experience that only older generations can provide. After all, changing the world is a big task and no one wants to be limited or to feel that their vision is being compromised. Let Millennials take on more leadership positions and you will see that they are more than up to the task of transforming your organization or business with their fresh ideas and new perspectives. Tradition is important; the old ways worked for a long time. However, we are living in the "new now," a place that is unfamiliar, unstable, and fast-paced. Millennials alone understand the way through the maze of ever-changing technology, economic situations, and organizational goals. They can change the world – but only if others let them by supporting them and allowing them to grow – and flourish.

Danielle Shepherd

Chapter Eight

How Me! Becomes We!

I hope that I've already shown you how valuable Millennials, with their transformative narcissistic traits, can be in the workplace. Now, it's time to find out how that kind of transformational leadership can usher in a new era of growth and excitement in the workplace. Again, you will find that Millennials hold the key to this kind of big and positive change.

If we look at things from a historical perspective, we can see that the world we currently live in is one of great change already. In fact, things are constantly changing - sometimes more quickly than we hope they will or expect them to. Many people who are called 'successful' (by society's standards) share a common trait - perseverance. Transformative narcissists, for example, are not strangers to failure. What sets them apart from other personality types is the way they *handle* failure. They do not easily give up. They are resilient. They take each failure and learn from it.

Some people believe that narcissists are so self-involved that they are not capable of learning from their failures. Nothing could be further from the truth when it comes to transformative narcissists. Transformative narcissists have the ability to ignore all obstacles that come up in their lifetime. This is because they view these obstacles as part of their journey in accomplishing their vision. Don't get me wrong. I don't mean to say that transformative narcissists are incapable of recognizing obstacles – or that they simply ignore obstacles when they arise. Instead, they are simply not deterred or profoundly affected by the barriers that they face. They greet obstacles with a positive attitude, knowing that each one can be a life-lesson.

me! me! me!

Transformative narcissists learn and grow from their failures, which could be seen as obstacles. The ability to grow cannot happen without acknowledging failures that occur. Transformative narcissists must maintain their capacity to stay unafraid, undeterred, and unaffected by the obstacles that they encounter. If they let obstacles get them down, they will risk the chance of losing their ability to be productive.

This ability – the ability to face obstacles head-on and learn from them – is a crucial component to a transformative narcissist. A transformative narcissist believes that he or she, out of all other people, will be able to bring forth their vision and produce significant change. A transformative narcissist's passion makes them able to persevere, to get through anything that comes their way – and to lead others effectively. Their passion for their vision overrides any self-doubt that usually comes with failure.

What drives a transformative narcissist is their thirst for knowledge. The transformative narcissist, similar to the productive narcissist, has an unquenchable thirst for learning. It is common, in fact, for a transformative narcissist to seek out information about any subject that holds their interest. Transformative narcissists want to go beyond basic learning techniques. They want to not only read what is available on a particular subject, but learn whatever they can about it by *actively doing* – whether this is through literature, machines, or computers. Knowledge is essential for transformative narcissists to accomplish their vision. They tend to gravitate toward less formal and structured ways of pursuing their passions. They also tend to be, as we have seen, independent and to operate on their own terms.

As a leader, a person must gain knowledge that will be useful in accomplishing goals, regardless of personal interest. A transformative narcissist's determination to learn about things that are of interest to them is useful in acquiring their goals. Successful, transformative narcissists, for example, must learn to apply their voracious appetite for learning to all areas and subject matters that might help them bring their vision to fruition.

One of the other things that we have yet to mention about transformative narcissists is that they often have, surprisingly, a great sense of humor. Now, I don't mean that they are particularly good at telling jokes – although they might be. Transformative narcissists, like productive narcissists have a different type of sense of humor altogether. The type of sense of humor that a productive narcissist has is self-effacing. Successful, transformative narcissists cannot take themselves too seriously. Otherwise, they will find it difficult to get people to follow them. Humorless transformative narcissists, in other words, are less likely to succeed. A transformative narcissist that has no real sense of humor will not be considered a grounded person and will have trouble figuring out what people really think of them. Transformative narcissists also use humor as a way to acknowledge their vulnerabilities, keep their egos in check, and ground themselves in reality.

We already know that transformational leadership – the kind of leadership that is most likely to transform organizations or businesses for the better – is all about a visionary individual getting others to accept their vision and take it on as their own. This means that, as businesspersons, entrepreneurs, employees, and employers, we must seek out ways in which we can make thinking of ourselves as a community – as a "we." What we need to understand now is how the attitude of "Me! Me! Me!" actually becomes "We! We! We!"

me! me! me!

You already know the difference between people with narcissistic personality disorder and those narcissists who have a certain brand of healthy narcissism. You also know that these individuals make some of the most influential and successful leaders in the history of the world. It is their influence that makes them capable of bringing others together in meaningful and important ways and, it is this kind of leader that we need for the future.

In the working world, there are many people who think only of themselves. You may already know someone who has the attitude that they should "take care of #1." In the current high stakes business environment, there are many people who take this view. They believe that because the business world is seriously competitive, they must only act in such a way that benefits them. These people do not worry about the future of their organization or business, much less about changing the world for the better. They want to get ahead by any means possible – and you might think that this makes them narcissists. However, although these kinds of people may share some traits in common with narcissists, they cannot be productive narcissists or transformational leaders.

As we have learned, the hallmarks of a truly transformational leader are very simple. A successful transformational leader will have their own, unique vision – and be able to convince others to follow them in bringing it to life. They *inspire* others to work together to get things done and to make significant changes for the better. It is this inspirational quality (along with viewing obstacles as lessons, being able to learn and grow from failure, having a thirst for knowledge, and having a great sense of humor) that makes the difference in this kind of leader. A transformative narcissist has to *inspire* and *encourage* others in order to reach a high level of success. How do they do this? By making everyone around them feel that they are part of something larger than themselves. By making everyone feel like a "we."

This is a strange way to think about things. And it's even harder for the average American to think this way. Part of the American dream is being able to have the freedom to do, within reason and the law, the things that we want to. In organizations and businesses, this often means having the freedom to achieve as much success and wealth as possible. Americans also, however, pride themselves in being individuals. That's one of the principles that the United States was founded on, after all. The first people who embodied this spirit went to the length of having a revolution to protect their rights and individual freedoms. How can we ask people who value their individual identity so much to suddenly work together in new ways that might make them feel as if they are just part of a group?

Part of the answer is that, though Americans do value their independence and individuality, they also have a strong sense of community. They help their neighbors when needed and are more than capable of banding together – if they find the cause to be important. This is what happened during the Revolutionary War. Everyone from each of the original thirteen colonies came together and fought for their right to live in a place where they would be properly represented, could practice whatever religion they choose, and live their lives in as free a way as possible [those individuals who were granted such freedoms under the constitution]. It's no different today.

When visionary leaders are capable of creating goals that everyone can get behind, people are willing to follow. They know that their own interests are not really being covered over, but elevated for the good of the whole. This concept is harder to understand when we think of an entire nation, but easy to understand when we think of organizations and businesses. Businesses do not exist in a vacuum. They exist within societies that depend upon them. This is what is normally called 'stakeholder theory.' The idea behind it is that nearly *everyone* who lives in a community where a business or organization exists is *affected by it* in some way – be it in big or small ways. Let me give you an example of the kind of thing I am thinking of.

If you take a look through your winter clothes, I'll bet you'll find some fleece. If you own any fleece that is made by North Face, Patagonia, or Eddie Bauer, then the kind of fleece your favorite jacket is made of is likely something called Polar fleece. Now, polar fleece was invented and was originally made in the small town of Lawrence, Massachusetts. The company that made Polar fleece was called Malden Mills, a textile factory based in Lawrence. For nearly one hundred years, Aaron Feuerstein's family owned and operated Malden Mills. They employed most of the people, in fact, who lived in Lawrence, Massachusetts. People who worked at Malden Mills would, in turn, spend their money at local diners, movie theaters, and shops. The entire economy of the small town centered on the Malden Mills textile factory.

On a fateful evening in 1995, however, things changed forever - both for Malden Mills and for the people of Lawrence, Massachusetts. One of the boilers exploded and caused a fire that destroyed the entire factory. When that happened, Aaron Feuerstein had a choice: he could either leave all of his employees without jobs and without health insurance until he received his insurance money, and the factory was rebuilt (and he had no idea how long that would take), *or* he could take money out of his own pocket and ensure that his workers had what they needed while the factory was brought back to working order.

Famously, Feuerstein chose the latter. In an amazing and generous move, he paid all of his employees their full salary and maintained their health benefits for the three or so months that the factory was being rebuilt. He did this without having already received compensation from his insurance company after the catastrophic fire. Feuerstein did this because he understood that Malden Mills was the lifeblood of Lawrence, Massachusetts and that – without the factory – the place would eventually turn into the proverbial ghost town.

In the end, Feuerstein did not receive as much as he thought that he would from the insurance company and, not too many years after the fire, he was forced out of his position as CEO and the factory was relocated. There were other factors as well, like an unseasonably warm winter causing Polar fleece orders to plummet the same year of the fire. Even though the story of Malden Mills doesn't have a happy ending, we can still take an important lesson from the actions of Aaron Feuerstein. What Feuerstein had was a vision. This was a vision that was informed by his predecessors in the family business and by his concern for the people of Lawrence, Massachusetts where he'd grown up. He understood the value of people not only working together, but pulling together in times of crisis.

In this case, the fire would have heavily affected the people working at Malden Mills if Feuerstein had not stepped in with his own money. They would have immediately been out of work, had to find other jobs, or perhaps even move out of Lawrence in order to feed their families. Feuerstein cared for the people who worked for him and cared for his hometown. He did not want to see Lawrence become a ghost town or to fail those who depended on him.

And his decision inspires us today. When the factory was rebuilt, the workers were able to return to work without having lost any wages or health care coverage. They were invested in Feuerstein's vision to make Malden Mills the best textile manufacturer in the world. They believed in Feuerstein and trusted him because he was ethical and had values that they did not expect him to have. Those workers would have followed Feuerstein to the ends of the earth because they knew that he cared about their shared vision.

The real lesson to be learned from the Malden Mills case is that, in the hands of a productive narcissist who is also a transformational leader, individual interest becomes the interest of the working community at large. Although Aaron Feuerstein definitely cared about the people of Lawrence, it was not only for emotional reasons that he decided to keep paying his workers through the aftermath of the fire at the mill. He also knew that the entire economy – Malden Mills included – of the town depended on the success of the factory. Every single person living in Lawrence at that time, whether they knew it or not, owed some of their success to the fact that Malden Mills existed to employ a large number of people. The town simply could not exist without the factory.

A leader like Feuerstein, who some have also called an "ethical hero," is truly a transformational leader – and likely a productive narcissist. He was able to inspire the people who followed him and was not deterred by the failure of his efforts. Though the mill does not exist today, its memory persists as a shining example of what an *individual* can do to make a *community* of a business or organization.

me! me! me!

When we begin thinking of ourselves as a "we" instead of focusing on our own, individual accomplishments, everyone benefits. Ironically, it is the transformative narcissist who has the power to bring people together to work toward a shared goal. Strange, isn't it? But, it's true. Transformative narcissists are inspiring and self-confident enough to take charge when need be, maintain good humor about it, and push on through anything. They can *transform* not only the workplace, but how we *view* work in general.

In addition, we should remember that transformative narcissists do not allow the needs and success of individuals to be buried under what is "for the greater good." No individual successes are sacrificed for the good of the whole organization. Instead, leaders of this kind actually bring people together to work toward a vision. The transformative narcissist gets to do what they love – lead, inspire, think divergently, and be creative – while followers are also valued in the same way. The kind of "we" suggested here is not just a sum of the parts that we add together to make a whole. On the contrary, this kind of "we-thinking" is beneficial to everyone – leaders and followers alike.

Failure will happen in businesses and organizations. This is inevitable. No one can change that fact. What can be changed is whether or not we are willing to take big risks. Transformational leaders are willing to do just that – and bring everyone else along for the ride. They will inspire enough, encourage enough, and address individual concerns enough to make it work. And even when failure happens, it will lead to something positive. A lesson will be learned and growth will happen.

Remember, the primary responsibility of a transformative narcissist is that of a role model. People need someone to look up to and to lead them. Even very smart people like having direction and being managed well. We get a sense of security and satisfaction from knowing that we are doing what we are supposed to be doing and that we are all working toward a common goal. This is what happens when we see transformative narcissists (those who think of Me! Me! Me!) actually building corporate cultures that encourage "we-thinking."

Danielle Shepherd

Chapter Nine

Absurd Memes, Student Loans, &

Avocado Toast

Generation after generation, the American workplace has changed. Some would say it's changed for the better and some would say it's changed for the worse. What is clear, however, is that change is happening at a greater rate than it did fifty, or even twenty, years ago. The first step, they say, in solving a problem is admitting that there is one in the first place. The truth is, the American workplace needs saving – and fast. There are about 79 million Millennials currently living in the United States.

That's quite a number! Think of the fact that there are only about 48 million Gen Xers in the U.S. right now and you'll get the idea of how large of a group Millennials are. Advertisers and businesses know that Millennials purchasing power is about $170 billion and, by 2030, it is predicted that they will make up about 50% of the workforce. Sure, they like to have a sense of humor about what they see as the terrible state of things in the nation (and the world), and they have the reputation for choosing to buy their Starbuck's latte and avocado toast rather than focusing on saving. Still, they are upbeat, engaged, divergent thinkers, and creative leaders. Learn how to understand your Millennial employee or colleague, and you will find that they are a wealth of energy and ready for any task you put before them.

Currently, about 27% of Millennials are self-employed. Could this be because they have difficulty communicating with the older generations that they encounter in the workplace? In my own personal reflection, as an entrepreneur and business owner, I've found it easier to be creative and productive when I call the shots. My place in the construction industry is among mostly Baby Boomers and Gen Xers, while they are bursting at the seams with knowledge that they want to share, they are hesitant and, to some extent, afraid of change. Millennial entrepreneurs enjoy gaining knowledge but thrive on being able to create new processes on how to utilize and implement knowledge – it makes the work highly engaging. Older generations may view the idea of owning a business as your first job as overly ambitious, and brimming with privilege and self-entitlement, but in truth, it's just the Millennial way. It really should not come as a shock, when Millennials were raised on the mantras of "You can be anything you want to be if you just put your mind to it" and "The sky is the limit." Certainly, it points to their positive and healthy narcissistic qualities in the sense that they would rather work for themselves and pursue their own vision than work for someone else and be limited by someone else's vision. What would happen if older generations could tap into all the potential that Millennials like me have to offer? Wouldn't the workplace be significantly improved? I think that we can safely say that it would – and could – if only Millennials were properly understood and provided with the opportunities to build a better workplace.

Ultimately, Millennials can work productively and well with older generations – under the right conditions. However, Millennials are a generation of individuals where if they can't join your team, they will go out and create a bigger and better team just to prove a point. More than ever, it is important to turn our focus on closing the generational divide in the workplace.

This is the time to think of Millennials, not as you have before, not negatively, but as positive assets in your organization or business. As there are many of them, especially women, who are transformative narcissists, capable of effecting great change, they will be an important element in creating successful companies and firms in the years to come. Tapping into the Millennial potential is not going to be easy. With so many generations in the workplace, there has been a good bit of tension between Millennials and their older counterparts.

But why not start now? Let go of everything that you know about Millennials and help them to *grow*, to become the transformational leaders that we know they can be. Take a moment or two to understand the Millennial, and he or she will reward your efforts tenfold. The stereotype is that Millennials do not value experience. This is only partly true. What Millennials don't like is being treated like spoiled children instead of adults. All of the tension in the American workplace could be addressed if misconceptions about Millennials were laid to rest.

What do Millennials want to help them succeed? They want you to be honest with them, to tell them what needs to be done in order to get ahead. They actually *do* value your experience, but thinking that they don't is part of the problem. Millennials are, as we have seen throughout this book, narcissistic. But, that's not necessarily a negative thing! Transformative narcissists, as you now know, are the best kind of leader. They are the only kind of leader that can really make big changes work. This is not to say that Millennials are the only ones who can be transformational leaders. I only mean to suggest that, since there are so many Millennials who display the traits of transformative narcissists, we need to acknowledge that fact and support them in their efforts to keep up with the ever-changing world.

me! me! me!

If you're reading this right now in a coffee shop, in the bathtub, your front porch, or even your office, take the time to think of a Millennial co-worker that you know. How often do you dismiss what they have to say simply because they don't think the way that you do? Because they think in ways that are different from what you are accustomed? Millennials are reaching out to older generations, looking for answers, looking for advice on how to be good leaders. They want to know what you know. They also want to take that knowledge and turn it into a successful vision for the future. Millennials are revolutionaries in the sense that they believe in themselves. They have the self-confidence and drive to encourage people to follow them. Yet, they are often dismissed.

If you are a Millennial yourself, then you know that the struggle in the workplace is real. How many times have you heard that your generation is "the worst" or that you simply don't know how the world works? How many times have you heard that your generation has no work ethic, got too many participation trophies, and spends their money unwisely? How many times have you heard someone put down your degree and say, "Well, it wasn't like that when I was a kid?" You may find yourself frustrated with older colleagues and managers at work because they simply don't understand where you're coming from. They seem to want things to stay the way that they are.

The truth is that the American workplace cannot remain the same. If we have learned anything from the business scandals of the early 2000s, it is that we are in big trouble. The old way of doing things won't work anymore. "But," Baby Boomers and Gen Xers protest, "I was able to take care of myself and buy a house and raise a family. What's wrong with these Millennials?

me! me! me!

Why do they whine all the time about how bad things are? Can't they figure out anything for themselves?"

Yes. Millennials are well aware of the current state of the world – that's why they want to change it. They were told to get a college degree or else suffer the fate of flipping burgers for the rest of their lives. They listened to their parents, went to college, tried to get a degree that would get them a good job, and did everything they were supposed to do. Now, they are finding it difficult to find a job at all, even with a higher-level college degree (hence the stories about so many of them living in their parent's basements). If a Millennial is lucky enough to find a job after college, they will be tasked with spending 8 to 10 percent of their income on paying back student loans for at least the next 10 years.

Many Millennials will live at home because it is necessary for them to take unpaid internships. Why? Because any job they apply for requires a minimum number of years of experience. They are caught in a "Catch-22," damned if they do and damned if they don't. Millennials will respond to older generations' criticism by saying, "Why haven't you retired and made room for us in the workplace? Why do you think that the world now is the same world that you grew up in? Can't you see that there are no jobs for us to take? That's why we're drifting aimlessly from job to job and career to career – we have limited options!"

Whether you are a member of the Baby Boomers, a Gen Xer, or a Millennial, you should now understand how important Millennials are to saving the American workplace. Their skills are skills that will be needed in the times to come. Have you Gen Xers and Millennials out there ever tried to explain *anything* about computers or the Internet to your Baby Boomer or Silent Generation parents? It's challenging to say the least.

me! me! me!

Most of us don't like change, but change is inevitable. American ideals are changing as we speak. As mentioned before, there are many factors that have contributed, and continue to contribute to this change. Women are now a huge part of the workforce, diversity, and inclusion is now at the forefront of most organizations, and the economy is unpredictable at best. In each of our own generations, we knew what needed to be done in order to keep up with the times. Why is there so much resistance now?

Maybe it's because Millennials are misunderstood, but maybe it's also because the world changed – drastically – in the early to mid-1990s. Back then, Gen Xers were the first generation to spend part of their childhood with gaming systems and personal computers in the home. They were also the first generation of adults to have access to cell phones. Gen Xers, and previous generations remember when you had to leave a message on someone's answering machine and *wait* for them to get back to you when they could. Traveling down a long, dark road in the middle of the night and get a flat tire? Better walk to the nearest gas station or hope that a trustworthy stranger passes by – you couldn't just call roadside assistance or an Uber to pick you up! The world was much less "connected."

Smartphones, hand-held personal computers, iPods, iPads, medical advances, GPS navigation, digital forms of music, and social media are just advances that Millennials have grown up with – that older generations either did not have access to or had some access to later in life. Millennials understand these things in different ways than their generational counterparts – it's a foundational piece of who they are. Yes, they were raised to be self-confident and, perhaps, narcissistic. But that healthy narcissism will help them to become the leaders that the future needs.

me! me! me!

Narcissism has been branded as a negative personality type and the personification of bad behavior and poor leadership. There are only a small number of researchers who support the idea of healthy narcissism and only one who has labeled a healthy version of narcissism within the context of leadership as transformative narcissism. But, all the research that has been done shows that individuals with narcissistic personality traits somehow find their way to leadership positions. This is likely because of their level of confidence, divergent thinking, creativity, and desire to have their vision come to life. There is also evidence that organizations will seek out individuals with narcissistic personality traits without even knowing it - they are drawn to their charismatic and approachable personas.

My research has shown that there is evidence that productive narcissism is related and to transformational leadership - to create *transformative narcissism*. What we have learned is that productive narcissists do exist and when combined with transformational leadership, it can create transformative narcissism. When Michael Maccoby – a world-renowned psychoanalyst, anthropologist, and consultant first began looking into narcissism, he coined the term "productive narcissist" to describe narcissists that could embody and balance narcissistic traits and master productivity. As a Millennial, I have expanded on this theory and identified the capability of productive narcissists to also be transformational leaders – thus becoming transformative narcissists.

I hope that I have been able to liberate the concept of narcissism from the negative perceptions that people have. I wanted to show that productive narcissists, leaders with narcissistic characteristics, are the version of narcissists that are grounded in reality. Their vision is what is important to them – and they will lead others to help them to take risks, and to have the social intelligence needed to accomplish their goals. It is this "social intelligence" that makes transformative narcissists and transformational leaders different. They not only know what their own vision is and inspire people to follow it, but also bring about great change and accomplish great things.

There is, as we have seen, a new facet that we must add to our ideas about leadership – we have to propose a form of leadership that is not about the followers, but about the leaders themselves. Millennials have just enough disregard for social conventions and societal boundaries to make them uniquely positioned to take what has been done by older generations and improve upon it – in order to fit their vision into the "new now" that is constantly being created. For these leaders, and for this generation, success can be defined by how well their vision is brought to fruition. They are capable of bringing large groups of people together and directing them toward a positive, common goal. To implement change with the view of changing the world, a transformative narcissist has to come up with a strategy for everyone to be involved. This requires that an individual grows, but simultaneously gives him or herself up to the group effort.

Transformative narcissists engage with the passion of their vision; it is all-consuming, requiring the merging of their personal and professional lives. This unwavering devotion to a singular purpose is an unthinkable sacrifice for many. But, this type of devotion also brings about change and separates the transformative narcissist from other personality types. They are more prone, also, to grandiosity, self-focus, and self-importance. The most transformative of narcissists, however, are in complete control of their charm and charisma. This is part of what makes them good leaders – people *want* to follow them and admire them.

In the end, we know that things have to change, and as I said before, the American workplace needs saving. Who will save it? The transformative narcissists, the Millennials will. They will save it because they can and because they want to. They will come up with amazing and revolutionary visions of the future – and then implement these visions. Hopefully, they will also find that they have the support of the other generations that currently co-exist in the workplace.

So, the next time your Millennial co-worker sends you some meme that you don't understand, be patient. Know that they understand that their generation has been so heavily criticized that they will have to convince you that they are responsible adults. Don't assume, in other words, that Millennials aren't worth their salt. They are interested in their careers – and interested in knowing how to further advance. When you engage them, challenge them, and allow them to freely and creatively work toward their own vision, you will be amazed at what they can produce.

Just think of it! What if some of the Millennials you know were actually *passionate* about their work? What if growing Millennials' skills was the best way for your organization to advance? Think of all of the possibilities that could be right at your fingertips if Millennials, instead of being made fun of and criticized, were supported and mentored.

I have a friend who is the only Millennial in her workplace. She doesn't look her age and, so she has a hard time admitting to her co-workers that she is a Millennial. Why doesn't she let them know? Because, she hears too many terrible things said about Millennials on a daily basis. She knows, and I know, that Millennials are really not that different from members of previous generations. They don't all live in their parent's basements and spend too much time looking up cat memes and spending all their money on Starbucks and avocado toast. They are like she and I - and most of our friends. We are up and coming adults, trying to make it in a difficult job market. We have a vision, and we are eager to make sure that the world is a safe place for everyone. Sure, we think that there is some fault to be placed at the feet of previous generations for things like global warming and the economy, but we don't think about that on a regular basis.

We are the generation that will gladly take less money for more perks. We will do this because we want to believe in the job that we have. We want to be passionate contributors to the story of the American dream. More than anything, we want to *do something meaningful, and that affects big change.* However, most of the time we live normal lives - just like Baby Boomers and just like Gen Xers. We go to work, sometimes head to the gym, and have dinner with our families – whatever kind of families these are. We understand how important diversity, creativity, and challenging societal norms can be. In fact, we learned this from our parents and from Gen Xers that we know. Their passion has become our passion.

There's a musical artist who wrote a song a while back called "Waiting for the World to Change." In it, the singer talks about how his generation *wants* to change the world, but feels like they don't have the tools to do it. Millennials absolutely do not agree with this sentiment! If you want to change the world, you go out and do it. If you are unhappy with your situation or with the way things are at an organization or business, have the vision to make a difference and to change it, if not take your vision and build your own organization around it.

me! me! me!

We may have a hard time understanding how we got to this point in our society, but we are willing to take huge risks in order to solve big problems. In the workplace, we are no different. We want to make an impact on the world around us in so many positive ways, but often feel stymied by traditional ways of thinking, especially in the organizations and businesses where we work.

There is a better way. Millennials are currently poised to become the transformational leaders that they are meant to be. All they need is a little more understanding – and a lot of mentorship. So, please stop and think for a moment before you roll your eyes at your Millennial colleague across the way. I promise you that he or she is concerned with the same things you are. We all want to work hard, to have balance in our lives, to be happy, to make certain that the world is the way that we want it to be. We want to be understood and to have the support we need to grow and succeed. We aren't looking for handouts or waiting for someone to do our work for us. When we look as if we are attached to our smartphones, it's because we are trying to keep up with the fast pace of the world around us, to be informed, to try to be aware enough of our social and economic environment that we can try to figure out the best way to make change happen. We are the leaders that you are looking for – and need.

Transformative Narcissists, have been in short supply in the American workplace. Now, they are not only in great demand, but an entire generation of them is ready and waiting for their cue. Millennials are willing and able to take the weighty responsibility of leading the world into a new future head-on. We want to learn from you – and for you to learn from us.

Millennials really are the future. We are a generation of caring people who want to help others and see everyone succeed. We value diversity and fight against old societal norms like the binary understanding of gender and less progressive views of sexuality and race. We are concerned about the state of the planet and what will happen to it if we sit back and do nothing. We are highly educated; in fact, we are the most highly educated generation so far in the history of the world. We see things that others do not, dream and wonder about how to make our world a shared world – a better place for everyone in it. We worry about issues of justice and want to be the kind of leaders who will value ethical stances. We are not apathetic. Quite the contrary – we are concerned about respect and doing the right thing. We are a generation of people who would rather take the risk of fighting for what is right than stand with the status quo when it is wrong. We are, in a word, the heroes that can save the American workplace.

Danielle Shepherd

I know that members of the older generations will still smile, maybe secretively, at us when we do something or say something that indicates that we are Millennials. But, that's okay. Smile away! We know that our desire for change is not an *attack* on the way things were, but just a push to change them for the better. Americans will always believe that progress, in business and in life, is a good thing. Millennials understand this too, but they are more aware than any other generation about the need for things to change in the American workplace.

We are not worthless and lazy. We know about leadership and about how to get things done. We know this for the very same reason that older generations complain about us. We are, on the whole, narcissists. Yes. We admit it! However, we are the kind of narcissists who are healthy, well-prepared, willing to think outside of the box, are able to get others to follow through on our visions, and are hopeful about the future of the working world. Millennials may be worried about "Me! Me! Me!," but, if they are supported and allowed to grow, this "Me!" will become a "We!" that can save the American workplace, make it better for everyone, and usher us all into the "new now!"

Danielle Shepherd

me! me! me!

About the Author

Dr. Danielle Shepherd holds a Ph.D. in Organizational Leadership with expertise in Millennial Leadership and Transformative Narcissism from The Chicago School of Professional Psychology. She also holds graduate certificates in Cross-Cultural Management and Intelligence Studies. Dr. Shepherd has been a small business owner for nine years in various industries including construction and consulting. She most recently founded the Gens Y and Z Organization, a 501(c)3 established to educate at-risk populations on awareness and preventative measures concerning exploitation, sex-trafficking, and rape.

Danielle Shepherd

Notes

Chapter 1. Millennials are Bae

Page 1. *Narcissism in Millennials*: See Twenge, J. M. (2009). *The narcissism epidemic: Living in the age of entitlement*. New York, NY: Atria Books.

Page 2. *Generations in the workforce*: See Bennett, M. (2017, February 7). A Breakdown of the 5 Generations of Employees in the Workplace. [Blog post]. Retrieved from https://www.navexglobal.com/blog/formal-introduction-five-generations-employees-your-workforce

Page 4. *Visionary leadership and productive narcissism*: See Maccoby, M. (2003). *The productive narcissist: The promise and peril of visionary leadership*. New York, NY: Broadway Books.

Galvin, B. M., Waldman, D. A., & Balthazard, P. (2010). Visionary communication qualities as mediators of the relationship between narcissism and attributions of leader charisma. *Personnel Psychology, 63,* 509-537.

Page 4. *Studies on productive narcissism*: See Shepherd, D. (2016). *Productive Narcissism: An explorative correlational study of narcissism and transformational leadership* (Doctoral dissertation).

Chapter 2. Reflection Perfection: Into Narcissus' Pond

Page 9. *Productivity:* See Del Gatto, M., Di Liberto, A., & Petraglia, C. (2011). Measuring Productivity. *Journal of Economic Surveys, 25*(5), 952-1008.

Misterek, S. D. A., Dooley, K. J., & Anderson, J. C. (1992). Productivity as a performance measure. *International Journal of Operations & Production Management, 12*(1), 29.

Moon, M. (2009). Knowledge worker productivity. *Journal of Digital Asset Management, 5*(4), 178-180.

Page 9. *Narcissism in organizations:* See Bergman, J. Z., Westerman, J. W., & Daly, J. P. (2010). Narcissism in management education. *Academy of Management Learning & Education, 9*(1), 119-131.

Campbell, W. K., Hoffman, B. J., Campbell, S. M., & Marchisio, G. (2011). Narcissism in organizational contexts. *Human Resource Management Review, 21*, 268-284.

Duchon, D., & Burns, M. (2008). Organizational narcissism. *Organizational Dynamics, 37*(4), 354-364.

Page 10. *Narcissism as a personality disorder:* See Glad, B. (2002) Why tyrants go too far: Malignant narcissism and absolute power. *Political Psychology, 23*, 1-37.

Millon, T. (1996). *Disorders of personality. DSM-IV and beyond* (2nd ed.). New York, NY: Wiley-Interscience.

Ronningstam, E. (2009). Narcissistic personality disorder: Facing DSM-V. *Psychiatric Analysis, 39*(3), 111-121.

Page 12. *Psychopathy.* See Hill, P. L., & Lapsley, D. K. (2011). In C. T. Barry, P. Kerig, K. Stellwagen, & T. D. Barry, (Eds.). *Implications of narcissism and Machiavellianism for the development of prosocial and antisocial behavior in youth* (pp. 1-12).Washington, D.C.: APA Press.

Page 13. *Healthy/Adaptive narcissism.* See Hill, R. W., & Yousey, G. (1998). Adaptive and maladaptive narcissism among university faculty, clergy, politicians, and librarians. *Current Psychology, 17*(2/3), 249-262.

Page 14. *Narcissism within leadership and organizations.* See Campbell, W. K., Bush, C. P., Brunell, A. B., & Shelton, J. (2005). Understanding the social costs of narcissism: The case of tragedy of the commons. *Personality and Social Psychology Bulletin, 31*, 1358-1368.

Campbell, W. K., & Campbell, S. M. (2009). On the self-regulatory dynamics created by the peculiar benefits and costs of narcissism: A contextual reinforcement model and examination of leadership. *Self & Identity*, 8, 214-232.

Rosenthal, S. A. & Pittinsky, T. L. (2006). Narcissistic leadership. *The Leadership Quarterly, 17*, 617-633.

Chapter 3. True Vision: Narcissism Can Be Healthy

Page 20. *Normal personality development:* See Freud, S. (1914). *On narcissism: An introduction.* London: Hogarth Press.

Page 21. *Corporate culture:* See Eden, D. (1992). Leadership and expectations: Pygmalion effects and other self-fulfilling prophecies in organizations. *The Leadership Quarterly, 8,* 49-65.

Edwards, M. R. (2005). Organizational identification: A conceptual and operational review. *International Journal of Management Reviews, 7*(4), 207-230.

Kets de Vries, M., & Miller, D. (1984). *The neurotic behavior of organizations.* San Francisco, CA: Jossey-Bass.

Page 21. *Vision/Visionary:* See Maccoby, M. (2003). *The productive narcissist: The promise and peril of visionary leadership.* New York, NY: Broadway Books.

Sashkin, M. (1998). *Visionary leadership theory: A current overview of theory, measures, and research.* (Working Paper 96-121 (Rev. ed.)). Washington, DC.: The George Washington University, Graduate School of Education and Human Development.

Page 21. *Leadership effects on productivity:* See Avolio, B., Walumbwa, F., & Weber, T. (2009). Leadership: Current theories, research, and future directions. *Annual Review of Psychology, 60*(1), 421-449.

Lieberman, M. B., & Kang, J. (2008). How to measure company productivity using value-added: A focus on pohang steel (POSCO). *Asia Pacific Journal of Management*, 25(2), 209-224.

Page 22. *Traits of productive narcissism:* See Campbell, W. K., Goodie, A. S., & Foster, J. D. (2004). Narcissism, confidence, and risk attitude. *Journal of Behavior Decision Making, 17*, 297-311.

Judge, T. A., LePine, J. A., & Rich, B. L. (2006). Loving yourself abundantly: Relationship of the narcissistic personality to self and other perceptions of workplace deviance, leadership, and task and contextual performance. *Journal of Applied Psychology, 91*, 762-776.

Maccoby, M. (2003). *The productive narcissist: The promise and peril of visionary leadership.* New York, NY: Broadway Books.

Nevicka, B., Hoogh, A. H., Van Vianen, A. E., & Ten Velden, F. S. (2013). Uncertainty enhances the preference for narcissistic leaders. *European Journal of Social Psychology, 43*, 370-380.

Reidy, D. E., Foster, J. D., & Zeichner, A. (2010). Narcissism and unprovoked aggression. *Aggressive Behavior, 36*, 414-422.

Schwartz-Slant, N. (1986). *Narcissism and character transformation.* Inner City Books.

Page 22. *Narcissistic competition*: See Luchner, A. F., Houston, J. M., Walker, C., & Houston, M. A. (2011). Exploring the relationship between two forms of narcissism and competitiveness. *Personality and Individual Differences*, *21*, 779-782.

Ryckman, R. M., Thornton, B., & Butler, C. K. (1994). Personality correlates of the Hypercompetitive Attitude Scale: Validity tests of Horney's theory of neurosis. *Journal of Personality Assessment*, *62*(1), 84-94.

Watson, P.J., Morris, R. J., & Miller, L. (1998). Narcissism and the self as continuum: Correlations with assertiveness and Hypercompetitiveness. *Imagination, Cognition and Personality*, *17*(3), 249-259.

Page 23. *Understanding emotional intelligence*: See George, J. M. (2000). Emotions and leadership: The role of emotional intelligence. *Human Relataions*, *53*, 1027-1055.

Page 24. *Impact of visionary leaders on followers*: See Riesenmy, K. R. (2008). The Moderating role of follower identification in the relationship between leader and follower visionary leadership. *Emerging Leadership Journeys*, *1*(2), 62-77.

Page 24. *Charisma and narcissism*: See Deluga, R. J. (1997). Relationship among American presidential charismatic leadership, narcissism, and rated performance. *The Leadership Quarterly*, *8*, 49-65.

me! me! me!

Galvin, B. M., Waldman, D. A., & Balthazard, P. (2010). Visionary communication qualities as mediators of the relationship between narcissism and attributions of leader charisma. *Personnel Psychology, 63*, 509-537.

Popper, M. (2002). Narcissism and attachment patterns of personalized and socialized charismatic leaders. *Journal of Social and Personal Relationships, 19*, 797-809.

Page 25. *Success and failure of narcissistic leaders*: See Maccoby, M. (2007). *Narcissistic leaders: Who succeeds and who fails.* Watertown, MA: Harvard Business Review Press.

Page 26. *Sigmund Freud's take on narcissism*: See Freud, S. (1914). *On narcissism: An introduction.* London: Hogarth Press.

Page 29. *Organizational competitiveness*: See Iordan, M., Grigorescu, A., & Chilian, M. N. (2013). Competitiveness - productivity, sustainable development. *Valahian Journal of Economic Studies, 4*(1), 75-82.

Page 30. *The Narcissistic CEO*: See Brunell, A. B., Gentry, W. A., Campbell, W. K., Hoffman, B. J., Kuhnert, K. W., & DeMarree, K. G. (2008). Leader emergence: The case of the narcissistic leader. *Personality and Social Psychology Bulletin, 34*, 1663.

Chatterjee, A., & Hambrick, D. (2007) It's all about me: Narcissism CEOs and their effects on company strategy and performance. *Administrative Science Quarterly, 52*, 351-386.

Hoffman, B. J., Strang, S. E., Kuhnert, K. W., Campbell, K. W., Kennedy, C. L., & LoPilato, A. C. (2013). Leader narcissism and ethical context: Effects on ethical leadership and leader effectiveness. *Journal of Leadership & Organizational Studies, 20*(1), 25-37.

Resick, C. J., Weingarden, S. M., Whitman, D. S., & Hiller, N. J. (2009). The bright-side and the dark-side of CEO personality: Examining core self-evaluations, narcissism, transformational leadership, and strategic influence. *Journal of Applied Psychology, 94*(6), 1365-1381.

Waldman, D. A., Ramirez, G. G., House, R. J., & Puranam, P. (2001). Does leadership matter? CEO leadership attributes and profitability under conditions of perceived environmental uncertainty. *Academy of Management Journal, 44*, 134-143.

Chapter 4. The Workplace Generation Gap?

Chapter 5. A New Now: Leadership that Transforms

Page 45. *Charismatic leadership*: See House, R. J., & Howell, J. M. (1992). Personality and charismatic leadership. *The Leadership Quarterly, 3*, 81-108.

Howell, J. M., & Avolio, B. J. (1992). The ethics of charismatic leadership: Submission or liberation? *The Executive, 6*, 43-54.

O'Connor, J., Mumford, M. D., Clifton, T. C., Gessner, T. L., & Connelly, M. S. (1995). Charismatic leaders and destructiveness: An historiometric study. *The Leadership Quarterly, 6*, 529-555.

Page 49. *Trusting a transformational leader.* See Avolio, B. J., Waldman, D. A., & Yammarino, F. J. (1991). Leading in the 1990s: The four I's of transformational leadership. *Journal of European Industrial Training, 15*(4), 9-16.

Felfe, J., & Schyns, B. (2006). Personality and the perception of transformational leadership: The impact of extraversion, neuroticism, personal need for structure, and occupational self-efficacy. *Journal of Applied Social Psychology, 36*(3), 708-739.

Khoo, H. S., & Burch, G. J. (2008). The 'dark side' of leadership personality and transformational leadership: An exploratory study. *Personality and Individual Differences, 44*, 86-97.

Nielsen, K. & Munir, F. (2009). How do transformational leaders influence followers' affective well-being? Exploring the mediating role of self-efficacy. *Work & Stress, 23*(4), 313-329.

Podsakoff, P., MacKenzie, S., Moorman, R., & Fetter, R. (1990). Transformational leader behaviors and their effects on followers' trust in leader, satisfaction, and organizational citizenship behaviors. *The Leadership Quarterly, 1*, 107-142.

Tims, M., Bakker, A. B., & Xanthopoulou, D. (2011). Do transformational leaders enhance their followers' daily work engagement? *The Leadership Quarterly, 22,* 121-131.

Tourish, D. (2013). *The dark side of transformational leadership.* New York, NY: Routledge.

Chapter 6. Who Runs the World? ~~Boys~~? Girls!

Page 55. *Gender and narcissism:* See Grijalva, E., Newman, D. A., Tay, L., Donnellan, M. B., Harms, P. D., Robins, R. W., & Yan, T. (2015). Gender differences in narcissism: A meta-analytic review. *Psychological Bulletin, 141*(2), 261-310.

Heiserman, A., & Cook, H. (1998). Narcissism, affect, and gender: An empirical examination of Kernberg's and Kohut's theories of narcissism. *Psychoanalytic Psychology, 15*(1), 74-92.

Twenge, J. M. (2009). Status and gender: The paradox of progress in an age of narcissism. *Sex Roles, 61*(5-6), 338-340.

Watson, P. J., & Biderman, M. D. (1994). Narcissistic traits scale: Validity evidence and sex differences in narcissism. *Personality and Individual Differences, 16,* 501-504.

Page 56. *History of women in the workplace:* See Alonso-Villar, O., & Rió, C. d. (2017). The occupational segregation of African-American women: Its evolution from 1940 to 2010. *Feminist Economics, 23*(1), 108,134-134.

Fernández, R. (2013). Cultural change as learning: The evolution of female labor force participation over a century. *The American Economic Review, 103*(1), 472-500.

Page 57. Millennial women: See Shorrocks, R. (2016). A feminist generation? cohort change in gender-role attitudes and the second-wave feminist movement. *International Journal of Public Opinion Research, 30*(1), 125-145.

Page 61. *Women in technology:* See Clark, M. (2013). Gender gap growing for women in technology. *New Orleans CityBusiness.*

Clark, M., & Reporter. (2015). New Orleans setting pace for hiring women in technology. *New Orleans CityBusiness.*

Grove, M., & Smith, M. (2014). *It's time to remove the invisibility cloak from women in technology: Women in technology are largely behind the scenes and overlooked despite impressive contributions.* Washington: WP Company LLC d/b/a The Washington Post.

Chapter 7. Future Vision: Millennials Change the World

Page 67. *The Millennial workplace:* See Catano, V. M., & Hines, H. M. (2016). The influence of corporate social responsibility, psychologically healthy workplaces, and individual values in attracting millennial job applicants. *Canadian Journal of Behavioural Science, 48*(2), 142-154.

Campione, W. A. (2014). The influence of supervisor race, gender, age, and cohort on millennials' job satisfaction. *The Journal of Business Diversity, 14*(1), 18-24.

LaCore, E. (2015). Supporting millennials in the workplace. *Strategic HR Review, 14*(4), 155.

Lindorff, D. (2016). How millennials are changing the workplace. *American Banker, 126*(9), 16-18.

Walsh, D. (2015). Millennials in the workplace: For employers, words to the wise from the Y's. *Crain's Detroit Business, 30*(13), 11-16.

Espinoza, C., & Ukleja, M. (2016). *Managing the millennials: Discover the core competencies for managing today's workforce* (2nd ed.). US: John Wiley & Sons Inc.

Roberts, B. W., Edmonds, G., & Grijalva, E. (2010). It is development me, not generation me: Developmental changes are more important than generational changes in narcissism. *Perspectives on Psychological Science, 5*, 97-102.

Page 70. *Millennial diversity.* See Frey, W. H. (2016). *Diversity defines the millennial generation.* Washington: Brookings Institution Press.

Fast enterprises; fast enterprises recognized as a 'best workplace' for diversity, millennials and more. (2018, Feb 19). *Journal of Engineering.*

Essner, D. (2017). Millennials sound off on diversity in the workplace. *Public Relations Tactics, 24*(4), 7.

Donohue, M. E. (2016). The death of high performance programs: Transferring knowledge in the new millennial. *Journal of Diversity Management (JDM), 11*(1), 1.

Chapter 8. How Me! Becomes We!

Page 79. *Growth from failure*: See Stein, M., & Muzzin, M. (2018). Learning from failure. *Science and Children, 55*(8), 62-65.

Linacre, S. (2017). Learning from failure. *Human Resource Management International Digest, 25*(2), 40-42.

Ohanian, A. (2013, October 18). Millennials, turn failure into fuel. *USA Today*, p. 07A.

Page 80. *The work passion of a Millennial*: See Meiling, B. (2015). Changing the roles: Millennial women blend work, ideals and passion into careers. *San Diego Business Journal, 36*(46), 1-28.

Schmitz, A. (2017,). 'we're real and sincere' WV's youngest lawmaker says older voters inspired by millennials' passion, energy. *Charleston Gazette - Mail*

Chapter 9. Absurd Memes, Student Loans, & Avocado Toast

Page 92. *Student Loan Debt crisis*: See Landrum, S. (2017, October 20). The impact of student loan debt on Millennial happiness. *Forbes*.

Danielle Shepherd

www.ingramcontent.com/pod-product-compliance
Lightning Source LLC
Chambersburg PA
CBHW031926190326
41519CB00007B/432